Winning the Heart of
the College Admissions Dean

Winning the Heart of the College Admissions Dean

An Expert's Advice for Getting into College

By Joyce Slayton Mitchell

TEN SPEED PRESS
Berkeley / Toronto

Ten Speed Press
Box 7123
Berkeley, California 94707
www.tenspeed.com

Distributed in Australia by Simon & Schuster Australia, in Canada by Ten Speed Press Canada,
in New Zealand by Southern Publishers Group, in South Africa by Real Books, in Southeast
Asia by Berkeley Books, and in the United Kingdom and Europe by Airlift Book Company.

Cover and text design by Susan Van Horn
Illustrations by Ellen Sasaki

Library of Congress Cataloging-in-Publication Data
Mitchell, Joyce Slayton.
Winning the heart of the college admissions dean : an expert's advice for getting into college
/ by Joyce Slayton Mitchell.
p. cm.
Includes bibliographical references and index.
ISBN 1-58008-300-5
1. Universities and colleges—United States—Admission—Handbooks, manuals, etc.
2. College choice—United States—Handbooks, manuals, etc. I. Title.
LB2351.2 .M58 2001
378. 1'61—dc21
2001002642

Printed in Canada
First printing, 2001

3 4 5 6 7 8 9 10 — 05 04 03

Dedication

For my New Zealand granddaughter, Zena Marama Ngakura Mitchell Tei
Her best friends, Maya and Kiah
You are the first generation of truly globalized students of the world.
The world-view challenge is before you—Run with it!

Acknowledgments

The primary resources for *Winning the Heart of the College Admissions Dean* are the voices of my college-bound students from Newark Academy in New Jersey, the Nightingale-Bamford School in New York City, their parents, my college advising colleagues, my Fitzwilliam pals, and the college admissions deans and reps. I am indebted to each one of them, and I am thankful that these are the particular students, parents, and colleagues from whom I have learned and with whom I work.

I am grateful, too, to publisher Ross Connelly, Hardwick, Vermont, for the opportunity to reach out to rural college-bound students and their parents who read the "College Corner" column in the *Hardwick Gazette.*

With disappointed parents often at their heels, and the level of competition and stress for college admissions on a fast rise each year, it's hard for others to realize the depth of emotion and criticism that heads of school face in the reality of today's college admissions. I can never thank enough Allan E. Strand, former Headmaster of Newark Academy, and Dorothy A. Hutcheson, Head of School, the Nightingale-Bamford School, for always providing me with the support necessary to work creatively under these conditions. This support provides the resources for travel to every selective college in the country, attending the local, state, and national conferences concerned with college admissions, and hardest of all, encouraging my innovative ways to develop the college selection program at these schools.

It is a pleasure to thank Phil Wood, president of Ten Speed Press, for seeing the uniqueness and excitement of this book idea.

I can't imagine a career that has more rewards than working with teenagers as they learn how to create college options for their first year away from home. For living in this career, I am eternally thankful.

CONTENTS

PART II: Applying to College

INTRODUCTION

"I had a question, but now I've forgotten it" is what I hear most often from juniors and seniors who look in my door at the College Advising Office. "Step right across that threshold," I reply, "and I'll bet you'll remember it!" Sometimes students stand there for a minute or two before they remember two or three questions on their minds. The second comment I hear most often from seniors is, "Ms. Mitchell, wait until I tell you my dream about getting into college! You won't believe it—I dreamed it was raining college applications!"

How on earth do you suppose the college selection process got to be such a scary task? Was it always like this? Maybe you're like the high school students I know who ask, "Isn't there some way to make it easier?" "How do I know if I want a big college or a small one?" "Should I go to one in the North or South, East or West?" "Isn't there some way to get around all of this judging and evaluating by people who don't even know me and still have some dignity left?" No, it wasn't always like this. And no, there isn't any way around being evaluated by the dean. The good news is that *Winning the Heart of the College Admissions Dean* will help.

After being the college counselor at two Connecticut public high schools and two private high schools (one in New Jersey and one in New York City), writing a college newspaper column for the *Hardwick Gazette* in northeastern Vermont, and spending more than thirty-five years visiting and writing about college campuses, I decided to write a book for all of you college-bound high school students who want to get a handle on the process before everyone else tells you where to go to college. This book is also for those of you who don't have a counselor, teacher, or parents who know the college process. It's also for those of you who do have a college counselor but who want to get the whole picture of what's going on before you go into your own guidance office to ask your questions.

I have one goal for writing this book. And that is to help you understand the college selection process so that you will know that you are in control. Understanding the process makes it possible for you to make good decisions about where you are going to go after high school. You will learn how to evaluate yourself, how to research the colleges accurately, and how to win the dean's★ heart by communicating and personalizing those evaluations to the colleges. Throughout the college selection process, the emphasis will be on you, a particular student looking for a special college.

Seven Basic Assumptions

Over the many years that I have worked with high school students as they have chosen their colleges, I have developed seven basic assumptions and facts that are unique to my college selection program. *Winning the Heart of the College Admissions Dean* is based on these seven assumptions:

1. You are in charge.

The first basic assumption is that you are in charge. And that's new. Usually your parents and teachers have been in charge. They have had the last word. They know you. They know what's best for you. For the first time, *you* will have the last word. You are going to depend on how well you know yourself, and it's possible that some of your values are different from your parents' and teachers' values. You are going to have to decide what is best for you.

2. Make a friend of your advocates.

People don't know how they make decisions. We are going to build our program around the unconscious aspects of decision making, as well as what we do know about winning the heart. The second assumption is that no matter how you feel about them, you are going to make a friend of your guidance counselor and of the college representatives who come to your high school. Your guidance counselor will write your school recommendation to the colleges describing you to the college dean. The college dean is

★ "College Admissions Dean" or "dean" will be the term used throughout the book to represent any college admissions officer with whom you communicate. This could be the information officer on campus, the college representative who comes to your high school or whom you meet at a college fair, or the college admissions officer who answers your e-mail.

not going to call your favorite teacher or coach to ask them questions about your application; the dean will call your guidance counselor. You can't afford not to know—or to be less than friendly to—that counselor. Find out the name of the college admissions dean or college representative coming to your school, the so-called "designated advocate" at the college for your application. Start by knowing that person's name and how to spell it correctly. You can't afford not to know—or to be less than friendly—to your designated advocate at the college.

3. Choose eight first choices.

You can't choose your college until the college has chosen you. In the fall of your senior year, you are establishing options for April decision making. *You must choose where you are going from where you get in, not from where you applied.* You will prioritize your college list only *after* you know the decisions the colleges have made about your applications. That's a major difference. Your family and friends often don't take this difference into account when they ask, "What's your first choice?" Do not prioritize your applications—think eight *first* choices. When others ask, name your final eight—your "eight first choices."

4. SATs and ACTs don't get you in.

No SAT score will get you in. Harvard and Princeton turn away about half of their 800–800 perfect scores. Half. That's a lot of denial letters going out to perfect scores—not perfect applicants. A verbal 650 and a math 650 on your SATs won't keep you out of anywhere. Once you are in the SAT range of the colleges on your list, don't spend another hour and another dollar to raise your SATs an insignificant 20 or 30 points. Instead, spend your resources (time and money) in the classroom, on the playing fields, in the arts rooms, reading, and winning the heart of the admissions dean.

5. The college market is not a tight market.

The fifth basic assumption is that there are hundreds of colleges and

3

universities with different campus cultures and high academic standards all over America that you will love, that are a great match for you. Every high school student who takes the college prep curriculum will find many colleges who want him. Contrary to what you read in the media, there is no shortage of colleges. We have more than 2,400 four-year accredited, fascinating colleges and universities in the United States. Don't get stuck on having to go to only the few that you've heard of. What you must keep in mind is that you will like best what you know best. Therefore, your task is to know several best. Don't keep knowing one college better and better, because that's how you fall into the trap of "I've got to go to Dartmouth and only to Dartmouth." Ask yourself, "What is it that I like so much about Dartmouth? What else is out there like it, with less competition for admission?"

6. Personalize the process.

The sixth and most important basic assumption of *Winning the Heart of the College Admissions Dean,* and for you to repeat every morning while you are brushing your teeth, is this one: There are three major steps in the college selection process: (a) assess yourself, (b) research the colleges, and (c) personalize. But the greatest of these is personalize. Personalize. Personalize.

7. Be authentically and specifically you.

The seventh and last assumption to remember is that college admissions deans are looking for ways to choose one qualified student over another. They are looking for authentic applicants. Your task is to find ways to express your authenticity.

When the college selection job is well done, you will have several colleges to choose from in the spring of your senior year, several campuses where you will want to go. This book will help you develop your own list of colleges with your academic record and your interests, values, and aspirations in mind. Read this book thoroughly and refer to it often. Plan early, think carefully, and make the best use of all the resources available to you.

Remember that you are not in this college selection process by yourself—you're on a team. Your high school teachers, advisors, guidance counselor, principal, and coaches join you and your parents in working things out. They are your advocates. They will send your records and letters of recommendation, and they will highlight your strengths as they talk to the college admissions deans about you. They will help you gather the necessary information to make a good college decision. Therefore, while you're gathering the data about yourself and the colleges, think teamwork. You'll need advocates to help you get where you want to go. It's exciting to choose your college. It's a great adventure. Enjoy it!

How This Book Will Help

This book will expand your view of what's out there by teaching you to research the hundreds of colleges and universities in America that provide you with more options than students anywhere else in the world. This book will show you the specifics that the college admissions deans are looking for, so that you will learn how to best communicate who you are and why you want to go to their colleges. *Winning the Heart of the College Admissions Dean* was written to give you ideas and examples to describe who you are and what you want.

When I meet high school students in New York City, or northern Vermont, or Auckland, New Zealand, who want to go to college and who want me to get them started in the process, I always begin by having them tell me what kind of student they are. I want to know what they like to study, what they are looking for in a college, how independent they are, how much structure they like, how social they are, how interested they are in the performing arts, in sports, in reading. My purpose in all of these questions isn't to find "right" answers but to get them thinking in very specific terms. If a senior tells me that she swims, I ask her which events and how fast. It's not that colleges are looking for specifics in swimming, but they are looking for specifics in everything. Being specific and being authentically you are the only ways that you can separate yourself from your classmates

5

and the rest of the applicant pool (the group of applicants applying to the same college).

You are going to learn how to assess yourself and how to research the colleges. You are going to be making all kinds of decisions about which aspects of you to highlight on your application; you are going to decide which interesting specifics about you distinguish you the most. You are going to collect data about the different college cultures by reading about many, many colleges and listening to others talk about even more. Then in November or December of senior year, you are going to stop collecting more data about the colleges, and you will decide to which particular colleges you are going to apply. When a senior is working on his application and the question is, "Why do you want to come to Georgetown?" I don't want to be able to take Georgetown out of the essay and substitute Washington University and Haverford and have it work for all three colleges. Again, by learning to collect data on the campus cultures (life on campus), you will learn how the colleges are different one from the other. The college dean wants to know how well you know these differences. What is there about the match of that particular campus culture that you think will enable you to take most advantage of the opportunities they offer you there?

> Being specific and being authentically you are the only ways that you can separate yourself from your classmates and the rest of the applicant pool.

Learning your options is what decision making is all about. Knowing what's out there before you decide is crucial to good decision making. When the waitress asks you what kind of salad dressing you want on your salad, you have to know your options before you can choose. When your aunt asks you where you are going to college, you have to tell her that you're still researching your options before you decide.

In other words, the college selection process is a decision-making process. Unlike many other decisions, it's a tough process because it's so visible to everyone. Everybody wants to know, to compare, to judge, to give you advice and opinions. No future decision will carry the social visibility of the college choice. Your parents, brothers and sisters, cousins, aunts and uncles, neighbors and peers will ask, "Where are you applying? Are you applying early? Isn't that a party school? What are your SATs? Did you get in?" You and your family will often feel as if your whole identity is wrapped up in the names of the colleges to which you apply! Even though this is not true, it's easy to get carried away with this emotionally loaded process and to forget that your identity is based on so many more things than where you go to college. For example, your identity comes from where you live, from your high school, your parents' occupations and income, the level of education of your parents, your ethnic and religious backgrounds, your attitudes, interests, values, and ideals. Even so, never again will your decision seem so important to so many others. You will never again be asked to make a decision that everyone else in the world will know so much about. Social visibility is an extra burden of the college selection process.

Instead of the identity emphasis, let's focus on the educational opportunities the college selection process presents. Decision making for college provides a situation where you must learn how to distinguish yourself from your peers and how to highlight those distinguishing characteristics. This experience builds character and will teach you a process that you'll use all through life. It is an opportunity to learn about yourself and to develop skills to communicate that learning. You will get experience assessing yourself and expressing that understanding both in writing (application and essay) and in speaking (interview). Your college application and your essay are your chance to personalize and communicate your understanding of yourself in writing. Working out your decisions at home and school, discussing your self-assessment, and learning to highlight your strengths will build your confidence. So let's agree to turn the college selection process from an emotionally loaded, no-control, anxiety-ridden experience to a positive educational experience that will provide each of you an opportunity to learn more about yourself, to learn how to research about 10 percent of America's 2,400 accredited four-year colleges from which you have to choose, and to learn how to communicate your new self-awareness to get what you want—a college environment in which you will be most productive and happy.

The College Selection Calendar

No matter when you start thinking about where you are going to college, you can jump right into the college selection process by looking at the following calendar. Most of you will get into some kind of a formal program at school during your junior year. Or if your high school has a different college selection program, then by all means, go by your high school plan. For those of you who are starting your senior year, or even if you are halfway through senior year, always keep in mind that it's never too late to start the process. There are some colleges that accept students all through the senior year, and others even accept students in the summer after you graduate. So. Even if you've missed some of the testing deadlines, and you find yourself short on time to assess yourself and to research the colleges, know that it's never too late to get into college somewhere. For those of you who are starting early—in your freshman or sophomore year—your curriculum choices and grades in a rigorous curriculum will have the greatest impact on your college choices.

Freshman Year

Take the most challenging courses you can handle well: English, algebra or geometry, Latin, a modern foreign language, and a lab science, to include five solids if you are looking for a selective college in your future. Try several different areas of activities that interest you—sports, the arts, publications, leadership in student government and clubs, and community service—to figure out your interests and talents. Plan to take your biology SAT IIs and possibly math in June at the end of your freshman year.

Sophomore Year

Continue to take the most challenging courses you can handle well: English, the next level of mathematics, foreign language, and science. Again, take five solids if you are still looking for a selective college. Continue with the extracurricular activities that you found fascinating and start new ones if you have time left over from your academics. Take practice PSATs in October, and SAT IIs in June in chemistry and possibly in math.

Junior Year

September–June	▶ Meet with college representatives
October	▶ Take PSAT (all juniors)
February–June	▶ Meet with your guidance counselor to discuss college list
March–April	▶ Spring break: Begin college visits ▶ Write to your U.S. senator or representative if you are planning to apply to a U.S. military academy or participate in a ROTC program
May	▶ SAT I, ACT for all juniors, AP exams
June	▶ SAT II for all juniors (three are required by most selective colleges; three should be completed by June of junior year)
June–August	▶ Visit colleges ▶ Write college essay

Senior Year

September–November	▶ Balance college list of final eight with your guidance counselor
September–December	▶ Meet with college representatives ▶ College visits and interviews ▶ Student-parent college conference with counselor
October	▶ Notify guidance office and teachers of early application plans ▶ Take SAT I, ACT (another chance if necessary)
November	▶ Have teachers in place for recommendations ▶ Register for PROFILE ▶ Take SAT I (last chance)
December	▶ Take SAT II: Subject Tests, if necessary (last chance for repeats of English, math, science, foreign languages)
January 1, 15	▶ Deadlines for most college applications and FAFSA form
February 1	▶ Deadline for many college applications, college interviews
April 15	▶ Common college notification date ▶ Decision-making time
May 1	▶ Common reply date, deposit required AP exams
June	Yeaaaaa!!!!! Commencement

International Students: Welcome to College USA! Americans Abroad: Welcome Home!

International or American students coming home—colleges and universities in the USA are where students want to be. And you are just the student that the deans of admissions are looking for. Diversity is big in America. And the more diversity we can get from all over the world, the better we like it.

If you have been in an international high school outside of the United States, and if you are familiar with admissions to universities outside of America, you will find the American college application process quite different. The major difference is that once you prove your proficiency in English, American universities are concerned with more than just your test scores. Another difference for international students is that it's even necessary to win the heart of the college admissions dean! That is because the deans are not making their decision on the basis of your test scores. Instead, they consider everything about you, including your special talents and service to the community. Once you are within the curriculum, grades, and test range that the colleges are looking for, they will look at who you are, the student behind all of those numbers. In fact, the application process measures your character, your ability to write, your commitment to and passion for sports, community service, and the arts. All the parts of the application process that are described in this book are the things that you must pay close attention to. The dean of admissions will want to know how you fit into his campus community, what you can contribute to the health and growth of his particular campus.

> Diversity is big in America. And the more diversity we can get from all over the world, the better we like it.

Another difference in the American college admissions process is that there are more than 2,400 four-year accredited colleges and universities. Of those there are at least three hundred excellent academically strong colleges and universities all over the country that you may never have heard of—schools that are easier to get into than the popular ones. You can begin to learn about these exceptional colleges and universities in your research through the *Fiske* and *Insider's* guides described in chapter 3. The *Fiske* and *Insider's* guides that describe the American colleges deal with around three hundred colleges, that is, about 10 percent of colleges offering a baccalaureate degree. Don't get scared away by what you read in the media that it's impossible to get into American colleges. If you take away the 50 colleges most competitive for admission (not necessarily the best academically, but definitely the most popular), you will still have 250 excellent and interesting colleges by any way you want to measure: highly qualified professors who love to teach, a high percentage of students going on to graduate schools and top jobs in every career in the world, state-of-the-art facilities, great sports and arts programs, help with different learning styles, fabulous libraries, and high technology—all of the things that you have probably read about. What you may not have read about is the depth of excellent colleges and universities we have in America, and that there is plenty of room for many more international students. In fact, many deans of admission travel around the globe describing for you the reasons why you should consider coming to their campuses in all locations of America.

For Americans who are coming home from the Leysin American School in Switzerland, the Shanghai American School, the International School Singapore, the American School of Paris, or the English-speaking Merchiston Castle School in Edinburgh, Abbotsleigh and Ascham in Sydney, or the Diocesan School in New Zealand or the Ukarumpa International School in Papua New Guinea, chances are that you will probably have a college counselor at your high school who can help you through these steps and who knows what colleges your high school graduates have attended. Even though you have been abroad and don't feel up to date with the college scene, still, no matter what, you will be confident of your English-speaking competencies. Use this book to learn how to research America's great array of colleges and universities and to add the personalized application approach to better your chances for admission to your final eight choices.

Lucky for all of you that the college admissions tests, the SATs, ACTs, and the SAT II: Subject Tests are given in 180 countries all over the world. Follow the guidelines in chapter 2 for which tests to take when. In addition, if English is not your first language, you may be required, and it will be to your advantage, to take the Test of English as a Foreign Language (TOEFL), which is required by almost all of the colleges and universities in the U.S. The three sections of this multiple-choice test are listening comprehension, structure and written expression, and reading comprehension. Some colleges will require the Test of Written English (TWE) administered with the TOEFL, a two-page essay on a particular topic that is designed to test your writing ability. Still others require the Test of Spoken English (TSE) that measures your oral proficiency. You will read and listen to questions on a master tape and then record your responses. Even though a college does not require the TWE and TSE, if you are particularly good at speaking and writing English, take these tests anyway, and submit them as documentation of how good you are! Each college is different in their test requirements and it will be your responsibility to check with each college to which you will apply and ask for the testing requirements. Except in China, the TOEFL is offered only online. Check www.toefl.org for registration information.

Many colleges have a cutoff point for the TOEFL. Write or e-mail the dean of admissions to learn what the cutoff point is at the schools to which you will be applying. For example, you must have a computer-based score of 250 to get into Columbia, a 213 to get into Colorado College, and a 173 to get into the University of Oregon, just to give you an idea of the variation at three of our colleges.

As soon as the testing is out of the way, you will want to read and pay close attention to chapter 8 on writing the very important essay and chapter 9 on writing the application. Recommendations may be new to you, and when you read this section in chapter 9, notice what it is that the dean wants to learn about you from these letters. College letters of recommendation should be from people who know you well, not the big shots that know your parents well. The deans want to hear what your classroom teacher has to say about your learning style and your leadership in the classroom. Letters from coaches and the performing arts teachers should describe at what level you perform in athletics or the arts—your responsibility, leadership, and your character. Before you give the recommendation form to your teachers, show them the teacher recommendation section in chapter 9, so that they will see in what areas the dean of admissions wants to learn more. Remember that you have to win the heart of the admissions dean from afar—remember too, it can be done!

Financial aid is definitely different for international students than it is for U.S. citizens. In fact, many colleges have a cap on how much financial aid they can offer to international students. Read chapter 6—College Economics 101. How you finance your education is a concern you will want to raise early in the application process if you are dependent upon American money to come here to college. For example, many universities give a maximum amount of money in financial aid to international students. Fifteen thousand dollars is high. On the other hand, financial aid to international students has changed drastically in the past year. For the first time, several colleges are not distinguishing between American and international students for meeting the financial need of the student. Middlebury College, Mount Holyoke, and the University of Pennsylvania, for example, are among those colleges. Recently, Yale University announced that it will extend its "need-blind" admissions policy to all foreign students seeking undergraduate degrees. Duke

> **How you finance your education is a concern you will want to raise early in the application process if you are dependent upon American money to come here to college.**

has just increased their financial aid to international students. Globalization has hit the financing of university education in America. Keep in mind, however, that accepted students must always document their ability to pay before they are accepted, no matter whose money it is.

U.S. laws for visas vary from country to country. Usually it is very easy to get a student visa once you've already been accepted at an American college. However, that student visa will not permit you to work in the United States. You will need a green card (U.S. government document) to prove permanent residency if you intend to work, although most of you will not be residents. Again, you have to check the visa laws according to what country you are from. Once you have been accepted by the college, the college will give you good advice on how to get your student visa. Look at it this way: It would be highly unusual for an international student not to be able to get a student visa once he has been admitted to an American college.

Think about the information you need about the college to which you are applying in order to be a success in your American experience. Find out if there are classes in English as a Second Language (ESL) offered at the college. If ESL classes are offered, how soon can you begin these classes? Is there special housing for international students? Most of you will want to be sure that you have campus housing before you get here. The college dormitories are where you will get to know the other students on a daily, informal level. Find out if there are special programs, clubs, and counseling for international students. Ask if there is a dean of international students where you can direct your questions.

Americans returning home: Your parents may still work and live abroad, but chances are that you've got aunts and uncles, grandparents and cousins in the United States. Write ahead to them and be sure they know you are coming. It may not sound cool now, while you're still at home with your parents, but by the time you are settled in and want a plan and some place to go for Thanksgiving, your relatives may look a lot better to you by then.

PART I

Developing Your College List

CHAPTER 1

Self-Assessment

You are in charge. O.K. Now what's being in charge going to mean to you? What does "knowing what's best for you" mean to you? What it means is that between now and January 1 of your senior year, you are going to figure out who you are, what you want, what colleges are out there, and how to win the heart of the college admissions dean (after you decide to which colleges you want to apply). Does that make sense? No one does a good job at anything if the task doesn't make sense to them. So. You are in charge, and every step has to make a lot of sense to you in order that you always put your best foot forward. In fact, the deans of admissions are quick to say that your best foot forward won't do it: You need to jump in with *both* best feet!

In order to do your best, you have to know that the college selection process is a three step process: self-assessment, college research, and communication. The first step is a self-assessment, or evaluation of your academic standing, your educational values, interests, and aspirations. You will use this assessment when you discuss colleges with your guidance counselor, your mom and dad, and your friends; when you write your college applications; and when you go for your college interviews. Rice University's former Dean of Admissions Richard N. Stabell cautions you to "be honest with yourself in your assessment." Don't kid yourself about the record you are "going" to have; look at the record that you have now as you evaluate yourself. Here are some questions that will get you started in your assessment.

Goals and Values

Think about it. Go beyond what kind of student your teachers say you are as expressed by their grades and comments. Get beyond what your parents—and your big sister—think about you as a student. Think about the questions below and add some of your own. Which subjects do you love or hate to study? How much time do you put in when you don't like the teacher? How influential is liking your teacher to the study time you put into that subject? Could you be working more? Are you sure? Do you want a college where you can take it easier than you have in high school?

> ► **What kind of student am I?**
>
> ► **What kind of student would I like to become?**
>
> ► **What aspects of high school have I enjoyed the most?**
>
> ► **What parts of school do I like the least?**
>
> ► **How do I define success?**

Students at my school have to work really hard. On the other hand, the work ethic is high and the majority get into it. They learn to love working hard. That means that after attending classes all day, and taking part in sports or plays or music after school, they get home around 6:30 or 7:00 and they have a minimum of three hours of focused homework. They often work their heads off and come up with Bs and Cs. No one at our school gets all As. Well, almost no one. Some years one student will end up with all As and A minuses. When I meet them as juniors I say, "Think about the college environment you want. What kind of kids do you want to be around? Who are your kind of people?" No curious student is happy at a college that doesn't have serious students. Even C and D students in some schools are intellectually curious, and they don't want a college where parties and sports are top priority.

On the other hand, I point out to them, they may not want to keep on working as hard in college as they did in high school. They might want to spend more time with their peers, in the arts or sports, or just hanging out for a change. In other words, don't assume that you want the same environment that you are used to, that your older siblings want, that your best friends want, that your parents want for you. There's an important book that will be very interesting for many of you to read as you think about what kind of student you are and want to become: *Colleges That Change Lives* by Loren Pope (Penguin, 2000). Consider what Pope says: "You're *not* as smart as you think you are if you believe: 1. Your college should be bigger than your high school. 2. A name-brand college will give you a better education and assure you success. 3. A university will offer you more than a good small college." And much more. His book goes on to describe forty fascinating campus cultures that accept B and C students and produce graduates who make a difference in the world.

When I first meet a new class of juniors at my school, I talk about all of these things, and then I ask each of them to write a one-page introduction of themselves to me, their college advisor, with whom they will be working until they get through the early, regular, or late-decision admissions process. (See chapter 9.) If you want to get started on this first step in decision making, go ahead, write a one-page description of what kind of student you are. Leave out your grades and talk about what you like and don't like to study. Everything you write will be grist for the mill. Those college applications and interviews are looking for your assessment of yourself. Knowing your goals and values will go a long way toward writing your application and winning the hearts of the college deans.

Academics

It is crucial for you to understand your academic standing in the college selection process. You should have a pretty good idea of what kind of a student you are and what your "numbers" are by the time that you make your final list of potential colleges. "Numbers" mean the strength of your high school curriculum, grades, where you are in your class, and your SAT or ACT and PSAT scores. If a college is on your final list, it's there because you've got the numbers—that is, you are academically qualified to go there. The best strategies in the world won't get you in if you don't have the numbers. Also, remember that at very selective colleges highly qualified students are denied by the hundreds. Princeton's Dean of Admissions Fred A. Hargadon frightens his audiences when he tells them that Princeton turns away two-thirds of the valedictorians who apply. All of the Ivy deans turn away more than half of the valedictorians who apply. Valedictorians!

> ▶ **What are my favorite and least favorite courses?**
>
> ▶ **What do I choose to learn when I learn on my own?**
>
> ▶ **Do my grades reflect my ability and potential? Why or why not?**
>
> ▶ **How well has my high school prepared me for college?**
>
> ▶ **Are my SAT scores an accurate measure of my ability?**
>
> ▶ **What is the average number of hours I study each night?**

We are talking here about winning the heart of the college deans for qualified students, where as few as 10 percent (Harvard and Princeton) or where 10 to 20 percent of the qualified students may get in (Columbia, Stanford, Yale, Brown, California Institute of Technology, Massachusetts Institute of Technology). You will need to use all of your time, energy, and money winning the heart of the dean at a college where you do have the numbers, so don't even think of winning a heart where you don't qualify. There are always a few students in every class who think that even though they don't yet have the grades and SATs that Ivy demands, they are so exceptional in other ways that they will get in. And it's very easy to find people who will take your time and money to affirm your belief. After all, you must remember that getting into college is big business in America. When someone is going to help you, notice if she is from your high school, an alumna or alumnus of the college, an SAT tutor, private consultant, and if the advice comes from a profit or nonprofit source. No matter who tells you what's best for you in your college admissions process—or any other decision such as traveling abroad, choosing a movie, buying Nikes—always notice what's in it for them to give you that advice. While we are on that subject, always keep in mind that the college admissions office is the marketing arm of the college. They are after as many applications as they can get. Like coaches, they throw a wide net and their interest is their institution. Your high school teachers' and your parents' interest is you. Of course the deans are friendly and helpful, and want you to apply—that's their job!

Now, where were we? Oh yes . . . applying to college without the numbers. Let me tell you a story: No matter what I said, Jamie was sure that Amherst would take him because he was so crazy about Amherst. No one could possibly want to go there more than Jamie wanted to go to Amherst. As his college advisor, I could see that he was so far off base that he and his parents received one of the very few letters I send home to say that he was using poor judgment to apply early to Amherst. In fact, Jamie only had a 10 percent chance of getting into Amherst, and never in my twenty-four years of college advising has anyone with a 10 percent or even a 25 percent chance ever gotten in. He is a wonderful young man, teachers love him, and he has a passion for learning. When he gets a C or B– on an exam or in a semester grade, or a 600 instead of his 700 fantasized verbal score on the SAT, he gets right up, brushes himself off, and gets on with life. He is more resilient than anyone I have ever met. I love this kid. Everyone does. We all admire him and realize that nothing ever can keep him down. But getting into Amherst? Jamie didn't have a prayer.

It wasn't that he couldn't do the work at Amherst—of course he could, all of the students at a strong high school where 100 percent go on to competitive colleges can do the work everywhere. That's not the point! The point is that colleges are swamped with applicants who are in the acceptable range. Applicants with a strong curriculum, B average, and 650–650 or higher on the SAT amount to a lot of students—and within that range are a lot of wonderful kids. It's not "average grades–wonderful kid" vs. "top grades–jerk." It's not a case of whether the college wants the nicest kid in the world with a little less on grades and the SAT vs. great numbers and the most rotten kid in the world. Those rotten kids, jerks, and no-personality kids with the top curriculum, all As, and 800s don't get into Harvard, Princeton, and Stanford either!

So there is Jamie, the optimist, applying early to Amherst without a prayer of getting in. He goes merrily along in senior year and tells me about each time he goes to visit Amherst. He couldn't wait to report that an admissions committee alumna promised to get him introduced to the dean of admissions at a ball game. Just as I know he will, he keeps getting to know Amherst better and better. We all love best what we know best. He handled the deferral in December very well. After all, he'll get in in April, right? Wrong. Now what's the danger here? The danger was and is that he never got to know the other colleges on his list. He didn't get into the schools where he had a 50 or 75 percent chance of being accepted. He had only one acceptance—at a school where he had a 90 percent chance of being accepted, but he hadn't even seen that school. Why not? Why didn't this great kid make it into the colleges where he had a 75 percent chance of being accepted? Because he "knew" he was getting into Amherst! Why didn't he have other acceptances from the less selective colleges on his list? "Because he showed almost no interest in our college," the other deans reported to me when I queried how they could possibly deny admission to this great kid. His teachers and parents were disappointed that Jamie didn't have more choices, but Jamie had cut off the possibility of other choices by being fixated on one college.

We all love best what we know best.

Clearly, the moral of this story is that it's important to keep searching and communicating with all of the colleges on your list. It feels very different in April to receive word about the college admissions decisions than you think it will in the fall when you are applying. It feels good to have April choices.

The Kid behind the Numbers

Right after the numbers, the dean looks at character. College admissions deans look for the strength of a person. Her integrity and maturity are judged by her activities, interests, and aspirations. Character and personality are not as easy to measure as the numbers in the academic arena. The measure that most deans find most important is how you spend your time when you are not in the classroom and when you are not studying for the classroom. Deans don't ask about sports only to find out if they can use you on their team; they ask you to find out what is important to you. When you have a choice to make about how to spend the next hour, the weekend, your spring break, your summer, what do you choose?

Dean Hargadon of Princeton is known for asking questions that will elicit character from his applicants. Even though all deans of admissions are after the same data, we know a lot more about how things work at Princeton than at most colleges because of a fascinating book that was written about the admissions process at Princeton: *Getting In: Inside the College Admissions Process* (Addison-Wesley, 1995). One of Hargadon's favorite parts of the application is his "hodge-podge" section. It's where applicants are asked to give their favorite word, time of day, newspaper section—little everyday things that fascinate experienced deans who have read thousands of applications from seventeen-year-olds.

> **The deans are always looking for the "you" behind the numbers.**

The deans are always looking for the "you" behind the numbers, and if you trust yourself enough, you can really have fun with this kind of section. Of course if you trust yourself enough, you can have fun with the whole process. One of the conditions for trusting yourself enough is that you don't "have" to get into a particular college. When you can be you and look with curiosity at many possible colleges all over the United States, then you don't feel that pressure of "Is this the right answer? Is this what they are after? Will the dean prefer this or that?" Trying to outguess what a dean will like turns the process into a nightmare and prevents you from being you. Having fun finding ways to express the "you" that your family and friends find so endearing is your task! Whoops! Off the subject again. The point is that when colleges ask about your activities, interests, and aspirations, the intent behind the question is, "How does this teenager distinguish herself when she has a choice in how she will spend her time?"

Activities, Interests, and Aspirations

The colleges want to know who you are. They will go into depth about asking you how you spend your time. In which activities are you involved? What form does your involvement take? How many high school years have you been involved in this activity/these activities? How many hours a week do you participate in this activity/these activities? When you are not in the classroom, what are you doing? The college deans will give you a rating for your activities.

> ▶ What activities do I enjoy most outside of the classroom?
>
> ▶ What do I give up in order to do this activity?
>
> ▶ Will there be time and opportunity in college for this activity?
>
> ▶ What do my parents expect of me?
>
> ▶ What do my friends expect of me?
>
> ▶ Who has influenced me the most?
>
> ▶ What kind of surroundings are essential to my well-being?

Now. Many of your parents get off base, way out in left field when it comes to activities. They ask guidance counselors and college deans, "What is the best activity to get into Washington U? What should she do in the summer to get into Bryn Mawr? Is baseball or lacrosse better to get into Tufts?" The point I want you to know is that the college wants to know who *you* are. Authentic you. What do *you* like

> **It's not what you do in the summer that counts, it's what you learn from what you do.**

best—baseball or lacrosse? What do *you* want to do in the summer? It's what you learn from what you do and how you express it in writing that counts most for getting into college. Cutting grass, being a mother's helper, pumping gas all count!

When Sally came in to tell me that she won the award in community service in her junior year and she was sure that would give her an edge, I had to admit to her that girls are big into community service and it does not always distinguish them. Now if she had a start-up computer business to tell me about, that would be a different story, because those young entrepreneurs so seldom are young women. If the guys come in with the community service award, that's another story too. So gender makes a difference in the activity. When you distinguish yourself, be aware of gender stereotypes. If you are a young woman applying to Bowdoin, Colby, and Vassar, where there are about four times as many women applying as young men, and your activity is community service, your interests are foreign language, humanities, and English, you have no edge at all—that's what the majority of young women look like, that's the profile. If your brother has the same record and applies to those colleges, his percent chance to get in will skyrocket! Your chances of getting in will skyrocket too if you spent your summers making a lot of money in some business that you initiated, love physics, and can't wait to take advanced mathematics. When you tell the college that you went to Chile or Nepal to do community service, they read that as "privileged." The summer programs at Harvard and Wellesley are not connected to the admissions office of the undergraduate colleges! Again, if you go to expensive summer programs, the first message to the colleges is that you can afford them. A parent once asked Dean Hargadon which activities would be most helpful in getting her son into Princeton—going to Harvard summer school, doing community service work in Honduras, or teaching English in China? The dean responded that the son should "pump gas." It's not what you do in the summer that counts, it's what you learn from what you do.

Personality, Character, and Relationship to Others

There isn't any part of the college selection process that the deans of admissions haven't thought through. They want to know your personality, your character, and how you get along with others. Harvard's Dean William R. Fitzsimmons is the first to say, "We look at everything. Everything." After all, it's of their community that you are asking to become a part. Another Ivy League dean believes that most teenagers nowadays haven't yet had many tests of character. He judges their maturity and integrity by the school letters of recommendation, what the student does in the summer, and in what kinds of community service the student has been involved.

If you only listen to the media and SAT prep people about the "numbers," I know it's hard to believe that what you do during summers matters at all. Here's a true story that will help. A top student with 750+ on more than five of her SAT IIs from a competitive prep school was turned down by Penn on the basis of her lack of interest in others. It's not that community service is the major criterion, but the lack of it can imply such self-interest that the college simply doesn't want such a self-centered person in their community, even if that centeredness is on mathematics and chemistry. So as you look at your application, realize that once your curriculum, grades, and test scores are established, the rest of the application is getting at your character, your belief system, your priorities—and nothing demonstrates your values more than how and with whom you spend your time. In thinking about the match between who you are and a campus culture, here are some questions to get you started.

> ▶ **What adjectives do I use to describe myself?**
>
> ▶ **How would my best friend describe me?**
>
> ▶ **Which relationships are most important to me? Why?**
>
> ▶ **How free do I feel to make my own decisions?**
>
> ▶ **How free do I feel to stand alone among my friends with a decision and point of view different from theirs?**
>
> ▶ **How do I feel about going to a college where the other students are quite different from me?**
>
> ▶ **How do I feel about going to a college very different from my high school?**

Many students aren't aware of what they are used to in their own environment because they haven't been asked to consider it. If they live in New York City and go to a small private school, they will often say, "I don't want a college that is too big after going to a small school all my life." And being from Vermont, I usually respond, "If a New Yorker can't handle big, who can?" There is a lot more to your environment than the size of your school. Look around you. What are you used to? How do you get to school? What is your experience with diversity in terms of race and economics? What is your neighborhood like? If you live in a suburb, your high school of two thousand is bigger than most liberal arts colleges. Are you looking for playing it safe or going after adventure? Are you a risk taker, or would you rather watch others go up on those high ropes? Knowing your own values can help you choose the college culture that is best for you.

How diverse is your high school? How diverse are your friends, is your community? Many colleges ask students to write an essay about the community in which they grew up. They want to know, among other things, how diversity (or the lack of it) in your community has influenced you. What does diversity mean anyway? Why is it so important, and why are America's top colleges fiercely competing for the diversity offered by underrepresented groups? First of all, education is following the global economic market and the Web technology. Educators strongly believe that students learn from each other. Therefore, the more diverse the college community, the more students will learn that diversity is the very foundation of today's age of globalization. You should know, too, that diversity means much more than the well-publicized racial and ethnic diversity. Diversity to the deans of admissions means all of the underrepresented groups in the world. These groups include first-generation college students; seniors from high schools not yet represented at their college; religious, geographical, and international diversity as well as racial and ethnic diversity. Just as the economic markets jump from country to country around the world, the American college dean recruits a student from here, another from there—rich and poor, high tech and low tech, from the Far East to the Southern Hemisphere, from Fairbanks to Sydney. American students have to look at the other side of the diversity issue as well.

Let's say it out loud: If diversity is in, privilege is out. Think about it: When the deans are searching the globe for the new and exciting, the privileged old tried and true *has* to be on its way out.

This change has probably been going on for the past ten years, but it's only recently that I have noticed

> Educators strongly believe that students learn from each other. Therefore, the more diverse the college community, the more students will learn that diversity is the very foundation of today's age of globalization.

myself saying to our seniors, "Don't write your college essay on your summer in Africa, in China, in South America. It just sends up a 'privilege flag,' and Fred Hargadon hates privilege!" That's a strong message from the Ivys. And it's a lesson that college advisors from the private schools from St. Paul's in New Hampshire to San Francisco University High School to The Lovett School

> **College admissions is big business in America today.**

in Atlanta have learned well. We have to take this lesson very seriously when we hear Tom Parker, the dean of admissions at Amherst, tell the parents of New York City's private school students that in his mind he deducts one hundred points from their SATs because they all have the advantage of so much SAT tutoring. Now that's an admissions dean's perception of privilege!

A college admissions representative from Washington University said to me that if the best schools of New York City could see the talents and achievements of Washington University's applicant pool from all over the world, we would realize that only the top quarter of New York's best students could stand up to the competition. And that's not Ivy or the Northeast or West Coast—that's Washington University in St. Louis, Missouri! As anxious as they are, many East and West Coast parents of college applicants don't even have a clue about that level of college admissions competition. Privilege from the strongest education program and private school legacy are no longer the qualities that the colleges value most. Diversity is.

Add to the diversity issue the facts that (a) college applications are increasing each year (1.5 million more college students expected to enroll by 2008), (b) the number of competitive colleges where the parents think their children "have" to go is static, and (c) the number of freshman in these colleges remains the same. It's easy to see that traditional, private school names no longer bring promises of Ivy admissions. Winning the hearts of the college deans by personalizing your applications becomes more important each year as thousands of talented and fascinating students from all over the world flock to America's higher education.

College admissions is big business in America today. What's big business in America? How about a $500-million-a-year college admissions business? And big business attracts the media. The media has jumped in and adds to the fear of your parents as they read so often about the so-called tight college market and necessity for SAT coaching at $100 to $400 an hour, and private consultants at $3,000 a shot or $29,000 for the "platinum package." Big business is visible to the media when they see the numbers of bookshelves devoted to the college selection process in the bookstores, not to mention the profits at *U.S. News and World Report* from their rankings enterprise. This is all new. We are talking only ten years of big profits—made on parent's anxiety and fears around the college admissions issue for their children.

As diversity and the media take over, the college market appears tighter and the college admissions process becomes more enterprising. You've got your work cut out for you on the diversity issue. If you are one of the underrepresented groups—black, Hispanic, or American Indian—be sure and acknowledge that diversity on your application. If you are one of the overrepresented groups—white or Asian, and women in many of the applicant pools—then start describing your diversity in other ways. Your primary responsibility is to describe your diversity in how you think, your style, interests, creativity, literary background, and leadership rather than being labeled as overrepresented or privileged because you are from an excellent high school.

Your primary responsibility is to describe your diversity in how you think, your style, interests, creativity, literary background, and leadership rather than being labeled as overrepresented or privileged because you are from an excellent high school.

CHAPTER 2

College Admissions Testing

Oh no—SATs! "Will a 1440 get me into Harvard? Yale? Cal Tech? I *have* to go to Brown or Berkeley or Georgetown. When should I take a course to raise my SATs?" My reply to anyone with a 650 verbal and a 650 math score and above is, "No, your test scores will *not* get you into Williams or Duke, but most important, those scores won't keep you out. And that's all you need to know about SAT scores. And that's all you need to worry about. Don't waste your time and resources worrying about SATs and ACTs, when there are so many interesting and exciting learning experiences in which to invest your energy!" Whether your scores are 650–650 or 450–450, you can be sure that a lot more than SAT or ACT scores go into the decision the colleges make about you.

Is there anything about the college selection process that makes you more anxious than taking, receiving, and sending your SAT or ACT scores? The worst part about this anxiety is that it's useless. Most of you have learned this fear through all the SAT prep companies and tutors, private college consultants and media who are making a lot of money on your fears. They lead you to think that if you only had twenty or thirty more points on an SAT you would certainly get into those very selective colleges that you are aiming for. In reality, test scores always disappoint. Remember that half of those 800–800 whizzes don't even get into Harvard and Princeton—because there is no score that gets you *in*. A better way to think about your SATs is what will keep you out. If you have a 650–650, you will not be kept out of any college in America because of your SATs.

> My reply to anyone with a 650 verbal and a 650 math score and above is, "No, your test scores will *not* get you into Williams or Duke, but most important, those scores won't keep you out. And that's all you need to know about SAT scores.

Let's take the bull by the horns right now and talk about SAT or ACT prep. When you think about it, the numbers craze on SAT and ACT scores—in the media and in your mind—is surpassed only by the way people talk about their weight. It's as if you *are* your test scores. Within this moneymaking SAT-prep machinery, numbers are easy to understand and to sell. But SAT numbers have been a best-seller in the media for so long, that you are believing the message. It may be easier to understand the relevance of numbers if we think of height and weight in athletics than test scores for college admissions. For example, we can all agree that even though an athlete's height enters into the performance of a basketball player and weight into the performance of a linebacker, most of us easily understand that the numbers, seven feet tall or 275 pounds, hardly predict a winner! And even though the speed of a tennis player's serve can bring her into the top competition, most of us cannot imagine choosing the U.S. Open champion by her hundred-mile-per-hour serve. We all know it's the personality and character behind those stats that makes a champion: motivation, coachability, discipline, attitude. SAT numbers are the same way. Test numbers are not *you,* and the deans of admissions are after the real you—the fascinating seventeen-year-old, with great character and potential for learning—behind those SAT numbers.

Now, how to do your best in the task you hate the most.

SAT Prep

Numerous studies on the effect of coaching on SAT performance have been conducted. There are varying conclusions derived from those studies, but virtually all indicate that becoming familiar with the test and developing thinking skills through the secondary school curriculum are the means of achieving significant improvement on SAT scores. Once you receive your PSAT scores, you often wonder if and when you should consider special review work before taking the SAT. Such work can take the form of individual commitment to build vocabulary and to take practice exams diligently in one of the many review books or courses available on the market. Some students choose to work with a private tutor or with a test review program. No matter what method is chosen, many of my students have seen score increases once they have made a commitment to take such work seriously. There are never any guarantees with such work since test taking is not an area where miracles occur, but if you feel anxious, know that you are being prepared for SATs every day in your rigorous high school curriculum as well as in your daily reading of the *New York Times.* The plan that is best for you depends on your history as a test taker, what scores you have now, and your own level of confidence in testing.

We do know that the SAT test is a reasoning test. Cramming the night before does not help. Instead of overwhelming your brain, get a good night's sleep. Be sure to eat breakfast. Prepare yourself for the SATs as you would for sports: Get in shape physically, intellectually, and emotionally! Students with the highest SAT I scores concentrate best for the full three hours. Others "get sick of the test," slow down, and often give up. Look at the clock. When you go into the third hour, eat some raisins or candy that you've brought with you. Psyche yourself up, tell yourself you are just as fresh this third hour as you were when you walked in. You're young: Three hours of concentration is easy at sixteen and seventeen! Chances are that you won't be devastated with some horrible score as they almost always are consistent with your grades at school. Remember that long-term grades count for more than one three-hour SAT I exam. Take each question as it comes and give it your best shot. The easy answers count as much as the hard ones.

For many of you, college admissions testing often began in freshman year when you took the June SAT II in biology. About 700,000 of you took the Preliminary SAT (PSAT) in October of your sophomore year, which is for most of you, the first major college admissions test that you took or will take. Sophomores headed for the most selective colleges have also taken the chemistry and math SAT IIs. By the time you are juniors, you will all take the PSAT.

Preliminary SAT (PSAT)

The PSAT is a short version of the SAT I: Reasoning Test. A record 2.25 million students took the PSAT in 2001. It measures verbal reasoning, critical reading, math problem solving, and writing skills that you have developed over many years, both in and out of school. You won't have to recall facts from literature, history, or science. You won't have to define or use grammatical terms. You won't have to write an essay. And you won't need to furnish math formulas; in fact, some formulas will be given on the test for reference. Sophomores take it for practice, but juniors take it to qualify (usually among the top 4 percent in your state) for the National Merit Scholarship Program. The PSAT recognizes outstanding black and Hispanic students as well.

If you are a learning disabled student, accommodations from extended time to special forms are available. Check out your questions with your guidance counselor or the College Board Web site. If you are an American studying abroad or an international student who wants to get an idea of the American testing system, the PSAT is given in most American and international schools. Contact the College Board through their Web site (www.collegeboard.org) to find out the closest testing site.

The SAT and ACT Tests

The SAT I is a three-hour test that measures verbal and mathematical reasoning abilities. The verbal section tests your ability to analyze reading passages, sentence structures, and connections between pairs of words. The mathematical section tests your abilities in arithmetic, algebra, and geometry. The SAT II: Subject Tests are one-hour tests in specific subjects. Subject tests measure your knowledge of particular subjects such as writing, foreign languages, mathematics, science, and history. You will choose which SAT IIs you will take.

The ACT, administered through the American College Testing Program differs from the SAT in that it covers four subject areas: English, Math, Reading, and Science. The ACT is more like the SAT II: Subject Tests than the SAT I. (Although coaches often think that their "athletes" do better on the ACT than the SAT, the selective colleges use a conversion chart to convert ACT to SAT score equivalents. Also, let's all remember that a few points on any test does not determine the college decision.) One of the main differences between the SAT and ACT is that the SAT has a stronger emphasis on vocabulary while the ACT focuses on grammar and punctuation. The ACT is all multiple choice, the SAT has "student-produced responses" in their mathematics section. The state universities in the South and Midwest most often ask for the ACT rather than the SAT. Whichever test your high school recommends is probably the one that you will take.

Registering for the SAT and ACT

You can pick up the necessary registration forms for your SAT I, ACT, and SAT II tests in your guidance office. (If your high school doesn't have the test forms that you want, check the College Board or ACT Web sites or contact them using the addresses in appendix B.) You will also need your high school CEEB code number for the SATs. Be sure to use the exact same name each time you register for a College Board test. The College Board's computer system sends all of your tests together only if you write your name and address exactly the same each time.

Score Choice

Score Choice allows you to put a hold on scores for all SAT II: Subject Tests you take on a single test date. Scores on hold are reported only to you and your high school. This gives you a chance to review your scores before you decide whether to send them to the colleges. Most juniors and all freshmen and sophomores use Score Choice, and release their best scores in senior year. It's important that you notice that Score Choice is great for freshman, sophomores, and juniors. It's another story for seniors. The deans of admissions at the selective colleges tend to agree with the Princeton Dean who cautions his applicants to think twice before using Score Choice as a senior. If seniors wait to receive their scores in senior year, and then ask the Educational Testing Service (ETS) to release those scores and send them to the college, the scores often arrive too late for the colleges to use them. Other times, students may forget they opted for Score Choice and just assume the colleges have the scores when they don't. Says Dean Hargadon, "Given that we [and probably most of the selective colleges] always use a student's three highest SAT II scores anyway, it isn't clear to us how the student ultimately benefits from this expensive option. What is clear to us, from this past year's experience, is that Score Choice exposes the student to the risk of not having a college receive his or her scores in a timely manner."

So remember these three things: (a) Having an incomplete folder is *not* the way to the dean's heart; (b) if you had hung around your high school guidance office last year and listened to the horror stories of seniors trying to get their SAT scores to the colleges on time, you would never use Score Choice in your senior year; (c) even if your SAT II: Writing score went down thirty points (which is insignificant on a 200 to 800 scale), the college is still going to see your highest score, so you are not taking a risk knowing it's the last SAT II you are taking anyway. The moral of this story is—don't even think of using Score Choice senior year.

Test Centers

Many of your high schools will not be an SAT test site, so you will need to register to take your SATs elsewhere. The SAT registration bulletin provides a list of possible test sites for your state. Look for the most convenient sites; you will be asked to list two choices. The earlier you register, the better chance you have to take your SATs in your choice of sites. Check out the dates and deadlines as soon as you know which tests you have to take. Juniors, you probably won't take any SATs until May of your junior year, and your SAT II tests are in June of your junior year. Usually the deadline for registration is about one month ahead of the test date. For example, if the SAT test date is May 5, the international deadline (that is, for international students and Americans abroad) will be March 27, and the deadline for students in the United States will be March 29.

Fee Waivers

Fee waivers are available for students who cannot afford to take the SATs. Your guidance office has the fee waivers and the guidelines for using them. Do not hesitate to ask for a waiver! Many counselors are far too busy to inform you of the fee waivers for SATs, college applications, and for the PROFILE, College Scholarship Service (CSS). Check with your counselor for the proper forms before you register for SATs or ACTs.

Nonstandard Testing

Nonstandard testing is helpful to those who have a diagnosed and properly documented learning disability or physical handicap. ETS offers extended time or untimed testing, and other accommodations for those who qualify. Talk with your guidance counselor if you have any questions about this testing option.

When to Take the SAT

Juniors will take the SAT I or ACT in May. Everyone will give you different advice on when to take your SATs. Let's remember that you are, like a scientist, learning to collect the data before making a decision. In this case, especially notice where the advice is coming from. If your SAT tutor says to take the SAT in your sophomore year, or January or March of your junior year, just realize what's in it for them for you to be taking it often. Some of your parents will think it makes sense to take the SAT during spring break when you aren't as pressured with schoolwork and finals. Just know that the research shows that the longer you are in school, the harder you are working, the more those little gray cells are putting in overtime, the better your test results. Being on vacation and relaxing is not the best time to take the SATs, even though it may first appear that way. Many seniors take the SAT I a second time in the fall or winter of their senior year, depending on their junior scores. The colleges will look at your test scores as late as March of senior year when making their decision (although you won't be winning the dean's heart by not having your tests there when they are ready to look at them). December of your senior year should be your latest date for taking college tests (although there are always exceptions to everything you are going to do in this process).

When to Take the SAT II: Subject Tests

SAT II tests are taken in June, in any high school year. Biology students in ninth and tenth grades are usually the first to take the SAT II: Subject Tests. A student takes the SAT II test whenever a course is completed, such as in biology or chemistry in ninth and tenth grades. Some math students take the math level I test as soon as they have completed algebra II and geometry. Most selective colleges require three SAT II: Subject Tests in addition to the SAT I. Juniors usually take writing, mathematics, and a third test on foreign language, science, or history. Doesn't that make sense? Now listen to a story, one of many "misguided advice" stories that I hear all too often.

Last summer a rising senior came over to my home to talk colleges with me. After talking a while about what she was looking for in a college, I commented, "With those grades in that tough curriculum, and those super SATs, you must have killed those SAT IIs!"

"I didn't take them."

"You didn't take them??? Didn't you say that you took honors biology in junior year?

"Yes."

"And you didn't take the SAT IIs when you finished the course??"

"No, my guidance counselor said to wait for senior year to take our SAT IIs."

"Does that make sense to you?"

"No."

The moral of this story is that no matter where the advice comes from, it must make sense to you! If you want to go to a selective college, take the SAT IIs in June of your junior year—it's a given. I don't care if it's the King of Siam who is giving you advice or the nicest guidance counselor in the whole wide world, if it doesn't make sense to you, ask again or ask someone else.

Seniors will take SAT II tests in December only if they need a third test or want to try for higher scores. There are eighteen different subject tests, and they are content oriented. They measure how much math, English, physics, French, or U.S. history you know. As such, they *can* and should be studied for. Each test lasts one hour; you may take up to three on any test day. Most colleges require the writing and math tests. Others require particular tests, and still others require none for admission. It is up to you to check out what each college on your list requires. How do you know which ones to take? Always take the writing and math. If you are in doubt about which level of math or which third subject to take, discuss your testing options with your teachers and guidance counselor. Your best bet is to consider your grades in the subject, your teacher's recommendation, and how well you do on a practice test, so that you will make a sound decision. You will find a practice test for every SAT II in a free booklet from the College Board, *Taking the SAT II*. Ask your guidance counselor for your copy.

Score Reports to Colleges

At the time you register for the SATs, you will have an opportunity to list four colleges (by code number) to which you can have your scores sent without additional fees. There is a $6.50 fee for sending scores to each additional college. *You,* not your high school, are responsible for sending your official SAT scores to your colleges. All of your SAT I scores go to the colleges. There is no Score Choice for SAT I scores. Most colleges use your highest scores, they usually look at the highest verbal and the highest math, not necessarily the highest set. SAT scores are mailed directly to your home and high school in about three weeks after the test is taken. Scores will also be mailed to the colleges that you designate when you register for the test.

> **NOW HEAR THIS!** Students must request that the Education Testing Service (ETS) officially send their SAT I and SAT II scores to the colleges. The scores on your transcript are *not* official. Your college application will not be complete until the college receives your SAT scores *directly* from ETS. (Seniors, does it sound like I'm making way too much of this little point? If you only knew how many seniors think that if it's on their transcript, they don't have to send it. Woe is me trying to get that second point across—you know the first point, right? SAT IIs in June of junior year, no matter what.)

Optional SATs

Some deans of admissions of liberal arts colleges are so disgusted with the $500 million industry that has grown around SAT prep and getting into college that they have decided to make the SAT I optional rather than required. Please read here, SAT I. Those same colleges still require SAT II: Subject Tests. And chances are that of the twenty or so colleges that do not require SAT I, at least one college on your list will require them, so don't even think of not taking them! That means that even if Bowdoin and Middlebury have an optional SAT, you probably have Colby, Colgate,

Hamilton, and a couple more on your list that do require it. So take the SAT or ACT. Decide *after* you get the results if you are going to send them to the optional colleges. The advice I give my students is that if you have at least a 550–550, send them, as the colleges will assume that your scores are much lower than a 550 if you don't send them. If you are one of the very few students whose top grades in a rigorous curriculum and SAT II scores are a hundred points above your SATs, then this option is designed for you! Here is the current list of colleges that have the SAT option, and it's growing: Bard, Bates, Bowdoin, Connecticut College, Dickinson, Franklin and Marshall, Goddard, Hampshire, Hartwick, Lafayette, Lewis and Clark, Middlebury, Mount Holyoke, Muhlenberg, St. John's College (MD and NM), Union, Ursinus, and Wheaton (MA).

The University of California has decided not to use the SATs because they believe the SATs are not a fair prediction of college success for everyone. Check the testing requirements for each of your colleges to be sure you comply. Every college is different and many change their testing requirements from year to year.

Advanced Placement Tests

Advanced Placement (AP) tests are given in May. These tests are designed to measure your mastery of college-level work in specific courses.

Even though most students take an AP exam at the end of an AP course, that is, a prescribed curriculum for a college-level course administered by the College Board, students can also take the exam without taking the course. For example, many competitive high schools offer a strong enough curriculum in English and U.S. history that students do well on the AP exams. The point of the exam is to earn college credits. For some students that means saving a year's tuition because they start college with thirty college credits, giving them advanced standing. Students who speak a second language, or if English is their second language, often take an AP test in their other language—Spanish, Russian, Chinese, Hebrew, or whatever their language is—without taking the AP course. As the scores are your own, you don't have to send them to the colleges, and if you have the $77 for each exam, many of you should go ahead and see how well you do. AP exams are scored from 1 to 5, a 5 being the highest score. Many students record a 3 and above (or 4 and 5 if applying to the most selective colleges) on their transcript for added documentation of their academic achievement. Senior scores on these tests have no impact on the college admissions process, because the test is given after all admissions decisions have been made. Enrolling and doing well in an AP course, however, will show up on your transcript, and of course a junior AP score of 4 or 5 is a strong academic credential for your college application. There is nothing that helps more in the admissions decision than doing well in AP courses, which are by definition the most rigorous offered at your high school. Key words here are "doing well." Taking APs for how they look on your transcript is not a sound principle for curriculum decisions. Many students are crying their eyes out in October of their senior year over the impossible AP calculus or AP biology course. They begged to get into AP European history because "I wanted an AP on my transcript" but are now getting a C– or D in the work. Qualifying for one course isn't the only question at hand; the balance of your whole course load also must be considered. Of course you can do an AP or two if that's all you have—but, no. You have a lot more, right? Listen to your teacher recommendations before you sign up for APs. Look at your exam score in the last course, not just your final grade, which averages in good homework and discussion in class. Never make a decision by how it looks to others.

What's Out There?
Researching the Colleges

H ow can you learn about all of America's colleges? How do you find the best match—the best college for *you*? Big or small, preprofessional or liberal arts, conservative or liberal, private or public, East or West—there are many things to consider. Looking at categories such as size, program offerings, philosophical or religious orientation, and location can be helpful, but categories and perceptions can at times be deceiving. In this chapter we'll look at ways to broaden categories and widen perceptions so you can find the best school for you.

Research skills are essential for making a good college decision. That means collecting data from a broad range of sources, looking at the data, and not being judgmental before you learn for yourself about the college. It's easy to go on hearsay. ("Someone told me that Williams is too small, someone told me that Michigan is too big, someone told me that UC Santa Barbara is a party school, someone told me that Grinnell is in a cornfield, someone told me that Rice is too hot, that Carleton is too cold, someone told me. . . .") It's easy, too, to say to your guidance counselor, "Give me my college list." Fortunately for you, good decision making doesn't work that way. Every college has something for someone. Every college is wonderful for someone. There is no college that is wonderful for everyone! Knowing you as you know yourself, there are many colleges where you will be happy (fit in with the other students, find the level of education you need and want, be productive, feel good on campus). Researching the colleges means finding several colleges where you really want to go. It doesn't make sense to have colleges on your list just because you can get in if you don't want to go there! You want to create a list of colleges where you *do* want to go. Of course you will want to go to some colleges more than others, but your research will open your eyes to new possibilities and options.

So, how can you learn about the colleges? To win the heart of a particular college admissions dean, you will have to know that school well enough to express why you are the best match for that campus culture. You are going to learn to research colleges from a great variety of sources. Most of you will have the opportunity to learn about colleges at college fairs as well as through college guides, college representatives at your high school, catalogs, college homepages on the Internet, view books, alumni, and college visits. Learn how to trust your own research. When you read or hear something about a college, notice who said it. Was it the college? What's their bias? Was it a student? What's his bias? Was it a college guide? Who wrote the guide: an educator, a student, an entrepreneur? What's in it for them? Why do they have a particular view of the college? For example, one of my high school seniors came back from a Tulane presentation at a New York City hotel and said, "I'm in love with Tulane; I just have to apply there!" Good for the college rep, he did his job well. His job is to get as many applicants as he can for his college class.

When you read or hear something about a college, notice who said it. What's their bias? Why do they have a particular view of the college?

You've been in science classes, at least two or three with lab work, right? You've taken social science, at

46

least history, isn't that right? Our model for learning about the colleges will be as a scientist—a social scientist, an anthropologist to be exact. An anthropologist studies human societies—different cultures, their daily behavior, ceremonies, language, food, families, relationships. All of these things come together and are called ethnography.

You are going to be an ethnographer in the field of anthropology and use the scientific collection of data to learn all you can about all of the campus cultures on your final college list. You have learned in science that you don't know the answer before you collect the data. You don't know the conclusion until you've done your lab work. Sometimes you work in teams, sometimes you take field trips. I take my junior class on a field trip to visit three colleges in the Philadelphia area: one large Ivy university, the University of Pennsylvania; one woman's college, Bryn Mawr; and one selective liberal arts college—either Haverford or Swarthmore—depending where we have the most students from our high school

> Our model for learning about the colleges will be as a scientist—an anthropologist to be exact. You are going to use the scientific collection of data to learn all you can about all of the campus cultures on your final college list.

that year. They read *The Fiske Guide to Colleges* and *The Insider's Guide to the Colleges* before they go. They learn to "see" the college campus, the campus culture. My students have already heard the names of these well-known, designer-label colleges. These juniors try to put all of that hearsay aside, as they go from one campus to the other to collect the data. They get a tour, an information session, and lunch with our own high school graduates who are now students on those campuses. You can do the same thing on your own with your parents and with other seniors in your class. Keep your answers and observations in a notebook—no one can possibly remember collected data for ten to twenty different campus cultures. Keep in mind that until you collect the data for all of your list, you are going to try not to judge the colleges. It's from your collected data that you will decide which eight colleges will be the best environment for you.

Research Questions

We start with four research questions: What's it like? Can I get in? How much does it cost? What will become of me? Let's look at each one of those questions now.

1. What's it like?

Here are the questions that you are going to be concerned with, the data that you are going to collect in order to decide where you are going to apply to college. This is the anthropologist part—the questions to help you measure the campus culture. You will look at size, location, number of students, percent of minority students, geographical percentages, percent of residential students, self-contained campus, beauty of campus, types of programs offered, athletic division, who you know there. You will ask how graduates from your high school do there. How large the freshman classes are, and who teaches freshmen. How accessible the college's libraries, labs, and computers are. Do you have to take math or foreign language to graduate? Is there a core curriculum? Is there a freshman seminar? What are the distribution requirements? Do they offer military training programs (ROTC)? Is there an internship program? How many freshmen stay for sophomore year (retention rate)? What percentage of the freshmen will graduate? What's the percent of students in sororities and fraternities on this campus?

2. Can I get in?

How selective is the college? Is my course load more demanding than most of the freshmen accepted? Is my record as good or better than most accepted? What is the SAT range of accepted students? Check *Fiske* and *Insider's* guides for selectivity information. What is the admissions track record of graduates from your high school who have applied there in the past three years? Ask your guidance counselor. Don't ask the dean of admissions what SATs are needed to get in—it's the number one question that they hate. Instead, ask the dean questions he loves, such as questions about the particular academic departments that interest you.

3. How much does it cost?

If it's a state university in another state, is it worth spending more money than my own state university? Does it sound better because it's somewhere else? Are the "public Ivys" (UC Berkeley, UVA, UCLA, Michigan, UNC Chapel Hill, William and Mary, UC San Diego, Wisconsin) a better value than a private college? Do I have a maximum amount I can spend? What are my parents willing to spend? What is the real price? Where can I find out more about financial aid? (Start your research with reading chapter 6—College Economics 101.)

4. What will become of me?

When the college reps come to your school and college fairs, ask about their graduates. It's a perfect question for the college interview. Most students are so intent on getting in that they never ask what will become of them if they attend a particular college, especially one they can't wait to go to. College deans love this question—it shows a lot of confidence on your part. You've gotten beyond the level of "Can I get in?"

Here are some questions—you will think of others—to get you started in exploring what will become of you after graduation: What do the graduates do? How many go on to graduate school? Which graduate schools do they go to? What kinds of jobs do the students get when they graduate? How many companies recruit on campus? How many graduates go into start-up companies? What percentage of graduates go to med school, business school, law school, schools of education or into Ph.D. programs? Where do they go and what are their fields of specialization?

Keep Your Eyes—and Options—Open

Big or small, East or West, hot or cold—where in this big country are you going to begin to look for a college? How far away from home you go depends a lot on your adventurous spirit and your feelings about weather. If you are considering even one university out of your geographical limits, then consider the whole country. Look and learn about all the best places that fit the description of the college that you seek. Students will tell me that they want to go to the Northeast, and then they add Lake Forest and Occidental. "But they aren't Northeast," I point out. "I know, but. . . ." If you're from the West and are considering engineering at MIT, then look everywhere! Look at Cornell and RPI in northern New York, Rice in Texas, Columbia in New York City, as well as Swarthmore and Brown, which all have engineering schools, and Carnegie Mellon in Pittsburgh. Don't limit your research by categories that may change before you have to choose your final eight.

Thinking about size, don't cut your initial possibilities too quickly by size. Numbers don't always tell the truth. Many juniors come in and say, "I want a medium-sized college, one with around five or six thousand students." Look through the guides and you will see that the majority of American colleges are small liberal arts colleges or big state universities. Stereotypes can be very deceiving. Big Wisconsin, Texas, and UNC at Chapel Hill students are not all numbers! The students on those campuses relate to each other and to their professors, and quickly break into small manageable friendship groups through living and learning groups and their special interests. A big university soon breaks down into friends from your sports team, music and theater groups, dorm-floor pals, suite-mates, sink-mates, political science class, lab partner or freshman seminar, so that you are not dealing with the whole university at once. The size of your high school has less to do with the ideal size of your college than your personality and what adventures you are ready for. Sure, you may have to take more initiative with that student-to-faculty relationship at a large school, but loads of eighteen-year-olds are ready for and capable of that! If a "family" community is important to you, think two thousand students and under. If diversity, high energy, and big-time sports are important to you, think over ten thousand.

If you want to check out majors by computer programs, you will miss the colleges who send the most students to business, law, and medical schools. The Ivys and most selective colleges don't have majors called premed and prelaw. In fact, graduate school deans get sick of reading all of those applications from chemistry and biology majors. They love to see an English major or an art history major who has taken enough chemistry to do well on the MCATs to be a shoo in for competitive medical school programs, or a Spanish or religion major who takes the LSATs and pops out of a pool of government, political science, or history majors for the best law schools. Besides, choosing a college by program is often misguided; students leave college because they don't fit in, which has nothing to do with program. Most importantly, "If the college does a good job with your education," says Theodore O'Neill, Dean of Admissions at the University of Chicago, "you will change your mind three times freshman year about what you want to study!" Let's take a closer look at all of the places you can research to learn more about what's out there.

> A big university soon breaks down into friends from your sports team, music and theater groups, dorm-floor pals, suite-mates, sink-mates, political science class, lab partner or freshman seminar, so that you are not dealing with the whole university at once.

Researching Campus Cultures

You will gather general data from outside the college before you turn to learning more specifics from the particular college sources.

College Guides

The bookshelves are lined with college guides. Begin your search with the best. Here they are:

The Fiske Guide to Colleges by Edward Fiske (Random House, latest edition). If you have money for only one guide, buy *Fiske.* This essay-style guide provides interesting information and evaluations for three hundred of the most selective and most interesting undergraduate colleges. It is an educator's view of the college culture and student life on campus. It's the best—read it! Don't take too seriously the SATs required to get in, or the rating of the colleges. Only your own guidance counselor will know which SATs, curriculum, and grades are acceptable from your high school to a particular college. It's the essay about the campus environment that is important in this guide. You'll start to get an idea of differences in campus cultures as soon as you read about several colleges. It's a great place to get an idea of what's out there while you are collecting data. The three hundred selective colleges in this guide represent the top 10 percent of America's colleges. They are all exceptional, and you'll see that you have a lot to choose from in terms of campus culture and selectivity.

The Insider's Guide to the Colleges (*Yale Daily News,* latest edition), published by students for students. Don't apply to college without reading this guide! It is student-biased, and it's definitely the next best thing to being there. College life and environment are the most crucial components of the college: If you don't fit in, you won't stay. The combination of educator *Fiske* and student *Insider's* is worth twenty visits to the college campus. Be sure to get an idea of "what it's like" to be on campus from this guide. Again, about three hundred colleges are described—the top 10 percent of U.S. colleges. There are a few different colleges in each guide as personal opinion varies, but for the most part they overlap.

The College Handbook (The College Board, latest edition). This is one of the most accurate and up-to-date "big" college guides available. The College Board collects the data each year, including which SAT tests are required by each college, from its own membership. Every college in the country is in this guide. *Fiske* and *Insider's* describe 10 percent of the most selective and interesting colleges in America. Those three hundred colleges, along with the other 90 percent of American colleges, will be cited in *The College Handbook*. Be sure and read the Student Life section; check out the percentage of students living in the dorms, the percentage belonging to fraternities, and the athletic division.

Hillel Guide to Jewish Life on Campus by Ruth Fredman Cernea (Random House, 2000). If you're Jewish or have a Jewish heritage, find out how many Jewish students are on campus before you decide to go there. You may like very few or a lot; the point is to learn if you will be one of a crowd, or if you will be known only as the Jewish kid on campus. This guide also describes the Jewish communities outside colleges that often invite college students to their homes for holidays.

The Multicultural Student's Guide to Colleges by Robert Mitchell (Noonday Press, 1996). This book includes information on what every African-American, Asian-American, and Hispanic applicant needs to know about America's top colleges. It includes campus culture, racial integration, ratio of men to women, numbers of multicultural professors tenured—the best guide of its kind.

African American Student's College Guide (John Wiley & Sons, 2000). This college guide comes from the nation's top African-American college guidance service, Black Excel. It is a comprehensive guide that describes the top one hundred colleges for African Americans and includes sections on finding the right college, getting in, and paying the bill.

International Student Handbook (The College Board, 2001). This guide tells international students what they need to know about ESL programs, required tests, TOEFL tests, application deadlines, international advising centers, and immigration regulations and requirements. It's as official as international students can get.

If you have any other special interests, check in your guidance office, in major bookstores, and on the Net for guides that focus on a particular topic. In addition to these cited, you can find guides for conservative colleges, athletes' colleges, historically black colleges, women's colleges, and more.

Finding Egalitarian Campus Cultures

The special-interest college guide that you will not be able to find is one for gay students (at this date, anyway). Because it's almost impossible for gay students to voice their concerns at school or to find publications for how to choose a college, the best advice that I can think of is to consider the qualities in a campus culture that all minority students must consider—mainly the egalitarianism of the campus. Let's look at some special considerations for gay students in choosing their campus culture.

If you are questioning your sexuality or are gay, you need to know what clues to look for in order to find the most supportive campus culture—or at least how you can keep away from the worst. We'll begin by looking at how other minorities figure out the best campus cultures to live in for four years. Certainly minority kids aren't all alike and don't want the same campus culture—what is supportive for one may not be the best for another. Some young women want to go to a women's college where they will get the most support as women. And yet, for many reasons, others don't. Some black students want to leave their suburban "white high school" environments and try Spelman,

> Kids aren't alike and don't want the same campus culture—what is supportive for one may not be the best for another.

Morehouse, Howard, or another supportive black college community for four years—still, other black students insist on integration. Some gay students will want to be in an environment with a strong gay community while others won't care. For the student seeking a gay social life, it's safe to say that the more egalitarian the campus, the more likely he will find it.

When leadership for student government and major activities are controlled by independents as well as by fraternities, the chances increase for an egalitarian environment. You should be very aware that big-time fraternities equal big-time trouble for minorities. Any campus that condones exclusivity in social life and student activities is not a safe place for the excluded. High school students certainly realize that popularity and exclusivity always hurt the nontrendy student. And in American high schools and college cultures, being gay, for example, is definitely not popular or trendy.

When a college has a history of admitting young women and blacks, high school students can count on finding a more open and supportive community for all minorities. Or consider the Ivys or state and private universities that are big enough to have large numbers of diverse groups on campus to form their own communities.

If you want to apply to a college where you have no idea about the campus environment, search out the egalitarian clues by looking at the *College Handbook* and the *Insider's Guide* to find the percentage of students in fraternities and the percentage of ethnic groups. Look in *The Fiske Guide to Colleges* to learn how much emphasis is placed on varsity athletics compared to the sports participation of students on nonvarsity teams. Read *The Insider's Guide to the Colleges* to get that all-important student point of view of campus life. All of these things together build an image of the campus culture.

Once you have a list of colleges, how should you present yourself for admission? How up front should you be about being gay? What will hurt your chances for admission at the colleges you want to attend? Should you follow the all-American model for the military and government service of "Don't ask, don't tell"? Within the application process, a crucial question

> When leadership for student government and major activities are controlled by independents as well as by fraternities, the chances increase for an egalitarian environment. Any campus that condones exclusivity in social life and student activities is not a safe place for the excluded.

that you have to ask yourself is, "Should I write about my sexual orientation in my college essay?"

Many parents of gay high school students and college admissions officers advise gay students to follow our current military model. This is what a gay college admissions officer told me. He said that he hears homophobic jokes about college essays all the time. "If I hear discrimination on gay essays at liberal Brown University, where they know I am gay, at a university which takes pride in diversity, just imagine what the consequences of a gay essay will be at conservative and preppy colleges." Listening to parents tell their story—and how long it took them to get used to the idea of their gay child—we learn that often their first impulse is not to pay for the education of a gay son. As harsh and immoral as it sounds to you and me, it appears that the advice that will most often help you at this age is—don't tell!

Even though writing often helps students feel better, it will usually be to your advantage not to write the college essay about being gay—just as other minorities don't get in by definition, even if they are a recruited underrepresented group. The key word here is *usually*. If you have been a gay activist in your school and have started, for example, a gay-straight alliance club like the students at East High School in Salt Lake City who after it was banned, carried their right to form a club all the way to the Utah legislature, then it's easy to see that writing about this experience will make sense. If you have been a leader in your high school's gay activist club, have demonstrated the courage it takes to take on such an unpopular role, and have stood up for what is not a teenage value, then you have truly distinguished yourself as a leader. Gay leadership is your strength. But if the essay is the more typical "poor me," "it's not fair" expression of a victim mentality, then most often it just won't stand up in the college essay competition. In those few moments when you have the focused attention of the college admissions dean, you must be highlighting your uniqueness and achievements as they will play out in the college community rather than focusing on your experience or feelings of discrimination or victimization.

When I hear parents of gay students say to high school students, "Don't tell parents, don't tell colleges," I listen. They are being practical and looking at gay students' immediate, short-term needs: getting into and through college before jeopardizing family emotional and financial support. However, James Gandre, Dean at the Chicago College of Performing Arts, former Dean of Admissions at Manhattan School of Music, and a leader in educating guidance counselors about gay students cautions, "Each student is unique and no formula, no matter how good or well intentioned, can be used for every student. If a student understands and accepts the risks he may face by coming out in an application, then the student has taken a bold and important step in meeting the challenges that at one time or another face all gay people in this not always so inclusive society."

Research those campus cultures carefully. Look for a history of egalitarian principles. Look for low fraternity numbers. Beware of what you are getting into. Your own perceptions of your sexuality and sexuality issues can change drastically in your first years away from home.

View Books, College Catalogs, and the Net

The first thing you receive from a college when you make an inquiry, visit their campus, sign a card at a fair, or score a certain number on the PSATs (whose lists are sold to colleges), is their view book.

View Books

Please keep in mind when you read view books, watch videos, and go online to college Web sites, that you are seeing through the marketing arm of the college and university. It's the hard sell with Madison Avenue marketing glitz. Don't even think of choosing your college because some college sent you a brochure and personal letter inviting you to apply! Go ahead and read them. If you can distinguish one college from another through their view books, you're good! Just remember this: Always question where your sources come from and what's in it for them. Some homepages on the Web are not produced through admissions, and often the student newspaper is on the Net. So explore those homepages to see what students say, and what they are doing and thinking about on campus.

College Catalogs

The catalogs are another matter. They provide you with the list of courses and faculty at each college without pictures. Students seldom look at them. I often put the catalog in their hands to answer the application question, "Why do you want to come to Colgate? Or Bates? Or Cornell?" The other time that seniors look at the catalog is when they are wait listed, and again, it's to their advantage to know the college in depth and to be able to explain to the dean why it's such a great match.

When I meet with my students to talk about researching the colleges, I take the first three college catalogs in sight and run through one department with my group. Let's do it. You're sitting there in a seminar room, we're all around a conference table. A couple of you are seated on the windowsills. In front of me are three catalogs: Goucher, Grinnell, and Guilford. Chances are that you may not have heard of any of these colleges, if so, good! That's the point: to get you to see many of America's outstanding colleges that you've never heard of. Let's say you are interested in theater arts. You know about the musical theater program at Syracuse, the acting program that takes only twenty students a year at

Carnegie Mellon, and you have a friend at the Tisch School of New York University who says, "Come here!" O.K. First we look at Goucher and we learn that it offers a theater major with six concentrations: general theater, performance, design and production, dramaturgy, directing and stage management, and arts administration. Next we learn that there are two professors doing all of that. Read through the course list and you will learn that there are twenty-four different courses offered in the department. Let's take a look at Grinnell's theater program, which is in the humanities division. There are six professors, although two are away on leave according to the catalog. Theater is an interdisciplinary major offering twenty-two courses including dance. Third, our last "G" catalog is Guilford's, where its theater studies program has three professors. Reading through this catalog you will learn that there are thirty course offerings, including dance and the history of theater. Do you see what's in the catalogs?

Go on into your guidance office after you have your final list of colleges, stand there for ten or fifteen minutes looking at the catalogs on the shelves, and flip through one particular department just to get the idea of what kind of a resource the catalogs are. There is no better resource for writing why you want to go to that college. You don't need to know what your major is going to be to profit from the catalogs. Take the high school subjects that you like best and look at the course offerings in French, gender and women's studies, and global development studies. What's that? Global development studies? Oh yeah, I see, at Grinnell they combine anthropology (we've heard of that before!), Chinese, English, French, history of South Africa, political science, religion, Spanish, and economics. WOW, I'd like that. Go ahead and tap the most underused, remarkably helpful resource in your college research: the college catalogs.

The Net

And now the Net. You'll find everything on the Net from registering for college tests to searching databases for a college list to scholarships to online applications. If you don't have the Web site of the college you want to research, both the *Fiske* and *Insider's* guides clearly include the e-mail addresses. E-mail the college and ask for its Web site address. If you don't have the guides with you, a good bet is this address: www. nameofcollege.edu. You'll come up with all kinds of information to get your search started. If your college is not listed in this way, try one of the college search groups and see what you get. My students like best the link they get from the *Princeton Review.* You can enter your preference, courses, grades, SATs, and the college search will come up with a college list for you. Here are some: *The Princeton Review* (www.review.com) has the easiest online application via Apply! Division; it also offers information about each college on your list. Check out *U.S. News & World Report* (www.usnews.com) for the latest ratings and message boards. CollegeEdge (www.collegedge.com), one of the earliest companies, includes college and scholarship searches. The biggest and most up to date is the College Board (www.collegeboard.com), which has all the general information you want to know, online applications, and college searches.

College Representatives Who Visit Your High School

Each year college representatives will visit many of your high schools. They come to talk about their colleges and to talk to you. *Go to those meetings.* It's an easy way to research the colleges. If you are a senior with a class when the college rep is at your school, and the college is one you are seriously considering, ask your teacher if you may be excused in order to see the representative. If you've already visited the college or had an interview at the college, you can say hello to the representative and relate your enthusiasm for attending the college. If you have an AP chemistry exam during the time the college dean is there, just zip by the college office to shake hands, say your name, and tell him that the AP chemistry is where you have to be. College reps love students to give priority to academics! A good impression, a face and name the representative will remember, and an informal meeting on your own territory go a long way toward winning the heart of the college admissions dean.

Your High School Faculty

College alumni are a valuable resource for learning more about a specific college. Ask your teachers to tell you about the colleges they attended. Some of your teachers will have graduated recently, but even though you may think that some of your teachers are too old to remember their college days, keep in mind that campus cultures don't change that much. Even though issues may be different, the preprofessionals vs. liberal arts, conservative vs. liberal campus cultures remain remarkably the same over the years.

College Visits

Spring break and summer vacation are good college visit times. Take the responsibility for arranging a family trip or a trip with a friend to see different types of colleges. You don't need to see all of the colleges on your list, as seeing some close to home will give you an idea for searching further. Senior year, however, is too late for all of your college visits. Colleges usually have students on campus the last week of August and the first week of September, a perfect time to see colleges with students there if your school hasn't yet started. In the next chapter, we'll focus our attention on how to visit a college campus.

CHAPTER 4

The College Visit

Visiting the colleges is the best. Seeing where you want to be a year from now and getting there is what this college selection process is all about. Remember the power is all in your hands, not the colleges', when it comes to you deciding where you are going to apply. The colleges will do everything in their power to get you to apply. Learning about the colleges will determine to which few of America's 2,400+ colleges you are going to send your strong, fascinating, unique, personalized application that will win the heart of the college admissions dean. The campus visit will probably have the greatest impact on your college choice. For that reason, it's a very important part of your college research. If your family is driving near any college campus, it's never too early to look. An unofficial tour of the campus, joining a group tour from the admissions office, sitting in on an information session, or just hanging out in the student union can be worthwhile to you before official visits start in spring of your junior year. Try for a variety of types of college cultures—big state, small liberal arts, conservative, liberal, Catholic, women's colleges—well, you know, if you're a young woman!

Scheduling the College Visit

Many a mother has called to ask me if she should schedule an interview when the family plans to visit colleges. My response is always, "I know how busy Jason is, I know that Julie is up to her ears in work, but the deans like to see the student, not their mother, take the initiative on college communications."

So, juniors, you can plan your trips with your parents, but *you* e-mail the college rep to set up your college visit and an interview. Or call the toll-free 800 number to make arrangements. (If you don't have it, get the phone number from your copy of *Fiske,* or call 800 information at (800) 555-1212.) Many, but not all, colleges have toll-free numbers.

How to See

Once you've got a college visit schedule organized, let's be clear about what you are doing there. What you are looking for in a college visit are the data that you can't learn from the guides, virtual tours, alumni, or college fairs. When I take a busload of my juniors to two or three very different college environments in April, I remind them that they are there as anthropologists, which means we are there to *see* what is. To see "what is" takes an open mind, a trained mind, a mind that collects data without judging, that collects data in order to find some solutions or results or conclusions only after all the research is completed. An anthropologist is the opposite of a person with a mind that has drawn the conclusions before he collects the data and goes to visit a college to affirm those prejudgments. Do you remember what anthropologists do? They study how human societies function. They observe how one age group relates to another (students to faculty) and what the food is like. They detail the daily lives of people, separating out work (classes), play (sports and fraternities) community government (student government), priorities of the group culture (humanities, sciences, religious, entrepreneurial, athletic, artistic, fun and games, service to others), the architecture (look of the campus), and clothing (What do the T-shirts say? What do students wear to class? Do they dress differently to hang out? To go out?). Anthropologists always study the family structure, courtship, marriage obligations, and sexual behavior (Do students date? Do they hang out in groups? Do they live together off campus? Do gay students have a place in the mainstream on campus? Are there many married undergraduates?).

As you observe campus life for your eventual judgment of the college, look for some common threads of what you like or don't like about the campus culture. Were there students you talked to that you would like to get to know better? Were there students who gave you new insights? Did they seem like your kind of people? Does this campus strike you as a likely place for you next year? How did it feel to walk into a classroom building? What were kids like to each other in the student union? What was the conversation about at the lunch table? One of my students was sold on Haverford when he scanned the bulletin boards outside the dining hall and saw a $5 bill posted with a note that said "FOUND—in stacks on third floor library!" Honor code on a daily basis was important to this young man. Seeing it in action, in addition to hearing about it in the information session, was very convincing indeed. Haverford was clinched for Michael when he met with students in a group session. He comments, "I've never heard such truth about a place, and ease for being excited about pure academics as I heard from that student session at Haverford last spring." Haverford's Dean of Admissions Delsie Phillips is the first one to tell students to look for the intangibles— the friendliness of everyone on campus, the excitement about academics— everything is grist for the mill. Michael is a good example of an anthropologist who collected his data from all of the colleges on his long list, applied to eight colleges, was accepted at half of them, and had a hard time deciding between two. He went back to visit the two in late April of his senior year, before he had to make his May 1 decision. But it was the data he collected from that college visit in his junior year, his first time on any campus, on which he based his final decision.

Trust Your Gut

It's often hard for seniors to trust their gut when on campus visits. They have heard so many one-liners that they aren't sure that they are seeing something different than they heard about. I remember a very funny, sophisticated young man who considered himself "the" liberal at traditional Newark Academy. Tom had the only ponytail among the young men in his class, played the guitar, and wore tie-dyed T-shirts under his collared shirt. He planned to apply Early Decision to Oberlin, sight unseen. He finally visited. While watching *Saturday Night Live,* he discovered that the group of Oberlin students were so P.C. that each one was offended and one by one left the room because of some ethnic or political joke. By the end of the show, he was the only one left in the room. Tom said that by the time his visit was over, he felt like a fascist! He forgot the Early Decision idea, applied to Vassar, and warned every junior he ever met to visit the colleges before sending a deposit.

When you think of how decisions are made, your unconscious should figure in. Your parents will understand that you can't always understand "why" you feel as you do. It's the same as when they first walk into an apartment or house when looking at real estate—sometimes one house or apartment will take right over—no explaining.

Collecting the Data

Can you remember everything? Of course you can't. And it would be impossible to remember anything unless you create a system to organize your evaluation of the colleges. You will want to have something simple that won't be too much trouble to fill out. (Well, some of you are more detail oriented and will want a complex evaluation, so go to it!) Add any other descriptions you read of the college. Include your own short list of things that are important to you so you can be consistent in your evaluation of each campus you visit. You can start to use it as you read *Fiske* and *Insider's.*

Check out the College Data Evaluation Form that my students use. Some use it exactly as it is; others use it to create their own forms, which match their curiosity and personality for collecting data.

COLLEGE DATA EVALUATION FORM

Name of College: _____

1. **What's most important to look for on this campus?**
   a) _____
   b) _____
   c) _____
   d) _____

2. **What's it like according to *Fiske*?**
   _____
   _____

   According to *Insider's*?
   _____
   _____
   _____

   According to me?
   _____
   _____
   _____

   What's it like according to graduates from my high school?
   _____
   _____

   Other students on campus?
   _____
   _____

3. Can I get in?

Curriculum requirements according to the admissions dean:

_____

_____

Curriculum requirements according to my guidance counselor:

_____

_____

SAT score range according to the admissions dean and guide books:

_____

SAT score range according to my guidance counselor:

_____

4. What I like most about it:

_____

_____

_____

5. What I don't like about it:

_____

_____

_____

6. What my parents think about it:

_____

_____

_____

7. Campus visit impression:

_____

_____

_____

8. Interview impression:

_____

_____

_____

Interviewer's name and e-mail address:

_____

_____

9. Can I pay for it?
Price per year:_____
Financial aid forms required: _____
Percentage of students receiving financial aid: _____
Average amount of indebtedness for graduates: _____
Director of Financial Aid:_____
Phone: _____
E-mail: _____

10. If I apply:
Enter college on your College Application Organizer chart in chapter 9.

Anthropologist in the Field: Observing the Natural Habitat of the College Student

If you lived in an ideal world and could collect all the data you wished you had for a perfect decision, you would stay overnight on each campus to learn what the daily life is like and what weekend nights are like compared to week-nights. You would take a late-afternoon guided tour, have dinner, and stay overnight with a sophomore. You would go to some social, ath-letic, or cultural event that evening. Then you would get all of your anthropologist antennae out to see what happens when everyone gets back to the dorm: Do they go to bed, sit around and talk, hit the e-mail, argue, get on the phone?

Campus Culture

Next morning you would attend classes and hang out on campus. You would talk to the faculty, see the coaches, eat lunch and talk with students, have your scheduled interview, take some notes, and leave midafternoon for your next visit at a college nearby.

That's ideal. No senior with a life can see many colleges in that manner. Do try, however, to visit a variety of types of colleges with the time that you do have, and try to see no more than two colleges a day. Be sure to take notes while you are there, or you will never remember what you saw where. If you have a short time, your minimum goal should be to take a student tour, attend an information session, and have an interview, if you have arranged it ahead of time.

Plan some time for the student union and talking to students not paid by the admissions dean, and look around the library to see who is there. In my many years of visiting hundreds of college campuses, I always head first for the library, to the reference section where daily newspapers are kept. Many, but not all colleges have easy chairs, couches, and wonderful places to sit down, put your feet up, and read your hometown paper. The newspaper section varies from only the *New York Times* and *Wall Street Journal* to fifty American newspapers plus the *London Times, Le Figaro* and *Le Monde* from Paris, *Republico* from Rome, and the financial news from Tokyo, Beijing, and Sydney. I am always curious about who is reading the newspapers, especially since it's a gender issue; over the years I would venture to say that the numbers of women I've seen in the newspaper section is one woman to one hundred men. Check it out! See what newspapers are subscribed to on the campus where you plan to spend four years, and see who is there reading them. And while you are in the library, check the rule on open or closed stacks (students respect the books enough to be allowed to be among them without restrictions) and check the hours—they will range from open twenty-four hours a day and seven days a week to closed on Saturday night and Sunday morning. Don't judge. Collect your data, and when you're going over your notes a few months later, your library visit may make a difference in deciding to apply there or not.

If you were on this ideal college tour, you would eat at least two break-fasts, lunches, and dinners to get a real impression of the food, who sits where, and what the dining hall behavior is like. When I went to visit one of my freshmen at Franklin and Marshall, she met me in the dining hall with "Hi, Ms. Mitchell, do you want to see where all the black kids sit?" Alicia, who moved to New York City from Puerto Rico when she was in third grade, is the kind of young woman who loves to get race in your face. And in fact, that is her distinguishing characteristic and why Franklin and Marshall was so eager to get her there: That's one kind of minority student that colleges search for, the one who gets the race conversations going whether students and faculty are ready for them or not. "Sure, Alicia, show me where all the black kids sit. Did you know that that is the name of a book?" So, juniors and seniors, look around those dining halls and notice if the athletes and fraternity broth-ers are all sitting in one place, if most students are eating alone, or if they are sitting in twos, or if they are at long tables with a gender and ethnic mix. What's it like? Remember you are looking for what *you* want to find there, not some combination that others tell you is best. It's your comfort level that you are after here. Just because you are a woman doesn't mean you want to be in a women's college or sitting with all the women in the dining room. If you are Hispanic, you may not necessarily want to find a place with great diversity; the strength of the chemistry department may be more important to you. "Diversity on campus"—the conversation of the moment. I remem-ber a black student from Newark Academy who was accepted at Princeton and Amherst, and while he wanted to go to Princeton, he was fearful of all the racist things he had heard about the campus life. Finally, he decided that the English department's strength was worth more to him than the lack of diversity on campus. Just because everyone is talking about it, doesn't mean that whatever the issue is, is the most important to you.

Take a Campus Tour—and Ask Lots of Questions

When you get to the college, arrange a campus tour. Look up some of your own high school alumni who are there. If you plan ahead, they will often take you to class with them. See your guidance counselor to find out who's there from your high school. When on the campus tour, be sure to ask the student guide as many questions as you can think of. Students are the best sources of information that you can get about a college culture.

Here are some questions that may get you started on your own student data collection:

▶ How large are your classes?

▶ Who teaches you? Can you get help from the professor?

▶ Who teaches the lab sections?

▶ Where do you study? Do you ever study in the library?

▶ Who grades your exams?

▶ Do kids talk a lot about grades?

▶ Have you ever been in a faculty home? How often?

▶ Do you talk much about national politics and issues?

▶ Do you belong to a fraternity/sorority? Are most of your friends in Greek life?

▶ Where can I get a copy of the campus newspaper?

▶ What do you like best/worst about being a student here?

▶ Where do most of the students hang out?

▶ What would you change about this college?

▶ What's the biggest student issue around here?

When you start planning your college visit, do not make the mistake of trying to visit too many colleges on one trip. Do, however, visit a variety of different types of colleges; this should help you clarify your thoughts in the decision-making process.

Before you get carried away with too much time away from school for your college visits, keep in mind that the most important thing you can do to get into college is to get the very best academic record that you can get. With your own academic record in mind, get out to visit as many college campuses as time and money will allow.

CHAPTER 5

Communications:
Personalize, Personalize, Personalize

Now here you are ready for step number three in the college selection process: communicating what you know about yourself to the deans of admissions in the colleges where you want to go. Think first that you will need a team to do the best job with these communications. Few students get into a highly selective college on their own. Finding advocates—someone to go to bat for you from your high school and in the colleges where you apply—is an important strategy that must always be in your plan to win the dean's heart. Your teachers, parents, guidance counselor, coaches, drama and music teachers, and the college rep are all on this team.

Communicating the Academic Record and Balanced List to Parents

Every spring, juniors at the schools where I have worked bring their parents in for a college conference. This occurs after spring break and before the end of their junior year. By this time, the junior has written a one-page self-assessment, has researched at least twenty colleges, and has visited two colleges with the class to learn how to "see" a new culture. Most have also visited one or two more colleges with their parents, attended a college fair, looked on the Net at the colleges' homepages, and talked to lots of seniors who know most about the colleges. Chances are, by the time the college conference rolls around, the students know a lot more about the colleges than their parents do.

In case you don't have a formal college program at your high school, let's run through this conference so that you get an idea of where you should be by spring of junior year. Here's what it looks like: We'll put Jake at the head of the table because he is the symbolic as well as true leader of the team helping him in his college choice. We begin with going over everyone's responsibilities in the college selection process, from spring of junior year until final list time in October of senior year. Jake's one and only responsibility, other than to do his very best academically, is to figure out what he really likes. The question he needs to ask himself with regard to each college is not "Can I get in?" but "Do I *want* to get in to this particular college?" His parents' responsibility is to help him keep an open mind, as everyone he knows and even some he doesn't know try to tell him where he should go to college. My responsibility as college advisor is to balance his list in the fall so that he ends up with eight applications to colleges he likes. These colleges will have a range of selectivity, that is, they will range from schools where he has a 25 percent chance of getting in to schools where he has a 90 percent chance of getting in.

Next, we go over his curriculum for his senior year, keeping in mind Jake's perception of himself as a student, which has emerged as he has articulated what he is looking for in a college and in his one-page introduction, which he wrote for me. By his grades and teacher comments and conferences, we know his high school teachers' perception of Jake as a student. The unknown factor is the colleges' perception of the student. How will the colleges look at Jake? Going over his senior curriculum is the best way to evaluate his academic record from the college dean's perspective. Jake is taking English, calculus, AP

French, AP Latin, and AP European history. The colleges will ask the college advisor, "Is this senior in the most rigorous curriculum offered in his high school? They will look at each subject and, with the high school profile in hand, see that AP English isn't offered, and all of the seniors take the same English, so yes, English is the most rigorous offered. The college dean will look for top mathematics, science, and foreign language.

In Jake's case, they will note that he doesn't have the top-level mathematics course and there is no science in senior year. "A verbal guy," they say to themselves. Back to our conference, we look at the PSATs. I'll comment, "If your SAT math doesn't get up to a 650, why not give it another try in December of your senior year after you've been in calculus class for four months?" Next, we go over Jake's long college list. He explains what he likes and doesn't like, and why. He tells us what he knows about each college and what his sources of information are. Jake and his parents are then advised to go forth into the world of college campuses and visit as many campus cultures as is feasible before fall of Jake's senior year.

Communication Means Personalizing

Personalizing the college selection process in this age of number crunching is the strategy that will most likely help you win admission over all the other qualified applicants. Personalizing the process is the strategy that wins the heart of the college admissions dean. In order to win that heart, however, you must first have the numbers so that the dean is interested in learning who is behind those numbers. There are two personalizing strategies for getting in where you want to go, strategies that you cannot do without. They are:

> ▶ **Make a friend of your guidance counselor.**
>
> ▶ **Make a friend of the college admissions dean (that is, the regional representative who reads and evaluates your application and comes to your high school).**

First, it is important to make a friend of your guidance counselor (college advisor) because she is the one who will be communicating (or not communicating) about you with the colleges on your list. No matter how inefficient, busy, or unfriendly your guidance counselor appears to be to you, you must make an effort to turn that around and make a friend of her. When the college has a question about your application, they will not call you, your coach, your outside consultant, or your favorite teacher—they will call your guidance counselor. You need her advocacy. The college process is a one-time opportunity. This is no time for attitude. The college selection process is the place where you will grow up enough to leave home. Making a friend of someone you don't know or don't especially like is a great leap toward the maturity and character you will need as soon as you leave home.

Personalizing the college selection process in this age of number crunching is the strategy that will most likely help you win admission over all the other qualified applicants.

Second, make a friend of the college representative who is responsible for your high school. In the fall, the college reps fan out across America and the rest of the world to visit seniors in their own high schools or in some central place where they invite students from all the high schools around. They go to Europe, Eastern Europe, Australia, New Zealand, South America, and Asia seeking the brightest talent and best mix for their next freshman class. Even if you have an AP calculus class when the rep is visiting your high school, if you want to go to Stanford, get yourself in to say hello to Robin Mamlet for five minutes, give her an academic reason why you love Stanford, and the academic reason why you can't stay to learn more. When you go on campus at Carleton and Dean Paul Thiboutot is in a meeting and can't see you, you leave a note and say, "I'm so and so, a senior from such and such, and I'm on your campus today. Sorry that I didn't get a chance to talk with you." When you live in Texas, and you know you aren't going to get a chance to visit Columbia, you call or write Director Eric Furda and ask who the representative for your Texas high school is. When you find out that Parker Beverage is both the Director of Admissions and the Colby rep for your high school, you become Parker Beverage's e-mail pal.

Making a friend of the college rep isn't just for the Ivys and small, selective colleges. College admissions people are interesting educators, they love young people, they want to build the best possible class. Get to know them! Win their hearts! Remember that they are going to choose a few from the thousands of qualified applicants who want to go to their college. The better they know who you are, the faster their hand will go up to vote for you around that admissions' committee table. Even huge public universities like Indiana, Maryland, Michigan, Virginia, and Wisconsin have a representative responsible for out-of-state high schools. Director Mary Ellen Anderson at Indiana calls high school seniors at home to ask if she can answer any questions about her university. Vice President and former Director of Admissions Linda Clement at Maryland sends personal notes to high school applicants. Ted Spencer, Dean of Admissions at Michigan, sends his admissions officers out to high schools with graduating classes of thirty as well as two thousand. Dean John Blackburn at the University of Virginia gives personal tours to parents and seniors who come on campus to see his university. Keith White at Wisconsin returns every phone call from every high school counselor within the day. There is no excuse for not making a friend of the college rep at the eight colleges where you will apply. Every letter, every classroom-corrected essay, every question, every e-mail, and every portfolio of photography or poems or short stories should be directed to this one person. Also arrange for your campus visit and interview through this admissions officer. You can't possibly win the heart of the college admissions dean without knowing his name or the name of your high school representative from each college on your list. Get those six or eight names from your counselor, or call the college admissions office and ask for the name of the college rep who handles your high school. Many colleges have toll-free 800 numbers. The toll-free directory for finding the college telephone number is (800) 555-1212. You can also use this number to request the e-mail address of the college rep for your high school.

What's the Dean Looking For?

When you communicate, when you write your applications, write your essay, and visit the campus for an interview, consider what the college deans are looking for when admitting their freshman class. While they differ in whom they take, they all use a similar basic yardstick in evaluating their applicant pool.

General Evaluation

Each applicant is evaluated by several readers within the admissions office and given an overall rating. The rating number is then brought to a committee meeting, where a decision is made by all of the admissions staff (these are the college representatives who come to your high schools, attend college fairs, and run the information sessions on their campuses). Before the admissions decision is made, the staff usually starts with evaluating six important parts to every applicant's file:

1. **Transcript**
2. **Test scores**
3. **Application and essay**
4. **Teacher recommendations**
5. **High school's recommendation**
6. **Other: interview, coach's ratings, special talent, outside recommendations**

Let's be clear about the evaluation of your file. As Duke's Director of Admissions, Christoph Guttentag, pointed out to me, these six parts are *not* equal; there is nothing that counts as heavily as your transcript, that is, which courses you have taken and how well you have done. Colleges put your academic work accomplished at the top of their evaluation process. Next are your test scores. Your SAT I or ACT scores, usually supported by your SAT

II: Subject Test scores have been verified over time as a reliable predictor of college success when evaluated with high school grades. Your application and essay are very valuable tools in the evaluation process. They show how well you write and how clearly you think. A creative essay can easily distinguish you from your classmates. Recommendations are very important, as teachers are the only people who have had direct contact with you as a student. They can write about your curiosity, motivation, dedication, effort, and all of those things that the dean is eager to evaluate. Because of that, you will want to choose teachers who you think will write the strongest recommendations you can get. Your guidance counselor's responsibility is to write a letter representing your high school that will summarize your academic work, speak of your personality, character, incorporate your parent letter if she has one, and highlight your special talents. Interviews, coach's ratings, activities, and special talent are usually important, but unless you are a national champion in writing, acting, linebacking, or cello, your extracurricular talents will never *substitute* for meeting the academic requirements the college is looking for.

Knowing what colleges "usually" do in the admissions process gives you some background for asking questions about the specific colleges that interest you. For example, even though many selective colleges evaluate in six areas, Richard N. Stabell at Rice University in Texas says that he is looking at five rating areas: the degree of difficulty of the curriculum, academic grades, school support (that means the guidance counselor's letter of recommendation), presentation (application, essay, interview), and personal qualities (character, maturity, judgment). At Rice, a regional college admissions officer first reads and evaluates the applicant. (The regional college admissions officer is the college rep who visits your high school, is at all of the college fairs in your city, and is your advocate in the admissions committee. This is the guy whose name and e-mail address you know because you are going to make a friend of him no matter what.) The second reader is someone who reads not by region but on a national level in order to get beyond the personal experience with the high school and student. When one of my students visits a college campus and comes back disappointed that he didn't get to see the regional officer who is responsible for our high school (but instead met someone else in the admissions office), I am always happy because it adds one more person around the admissions decision-making table who has met this student. All of the admissions staff have the same vote, whether they are regional director, dean, first year or thirty-fifth year on the job! And of course my student left a note to his regional rep saying he was on campus and gave some academic observation that impressed him while he was there.

Academic Evaluation

What does looking at and evaluating the academics mean to these deans? To give you a clear understanding of what the Ivys and their selective friends are looking for in their application pool of students from all over the world, let's take a look at the rating scale at Princeton, because (along with Harvard, Columbia, and Stanford) they've got the toughest of the tough for admission. If you know what Princeton considers a "one"—they rate on a scale from one to five—then you know the most rigorous scenario for getting in. When Dean Hargadon talks to juniors and their parents from the top New York City private (independent) schools, he says that he looks at the strength of the curriculum, the grades, and test scores. "A one," says the dean, "is somebody with five or six scores over 700 (SAT Is and SAT IIs), mostly As, a 4.0 average, and at least twenty solids. A solid means an honors course, or an AP course, or the most competitive level within the department." For example, some small high schools give only one English course, but if 100 percent of

> Admissions committees are always looking for the strongest points in your folder—things that set you apart from other applicants, ways that you distinguish yourself from your classmates. Your special talents are what make you interesting. Colleges look for a well-rounded class, *not* a group of well-rounded students. Distinguish yourself!

those students go on to competitive four-year colleges, that's considered a solid. On the other hand, if only 75 percent go on to a competitive four-year college, the course may not be considered a solid in Princeton's book. Needless to say, there are not many academic "ones" in any college's applicant pool. To rate an academic two, a senior must have twenty solids with a 3.9 average as well as five or six SATs over 700. Half of Columbia, Harvard, Princeton, Yale, and Stanford's applicant pool are usually twos or threes. It takes a one to distinguish oneself from the pack of twos and threes.

Standing Out: Special Talent

Special talent can make a big difference. We think of sports, because sports are often the most-talked-about talent, but each of you has some special talent that you will want to highlight on your own application. Some of you are outstanding musicians, writers, actors, poets, editors, photographers, and leaders. Others of you have a strong social conscience, unique hobbies, or an unusual background. Maybe being highly organized or committed to community service is your special talent. Admissions committees are always looking for the strongest points in your folder—things that set you apart from other applicants, ways that you distinguish yourself from your classmates. Your special talents are what make you interesting. Colleges look for a well-rounded class, not a group of well-rounded students. Distinguish yourself!

How does a student win the heart of the admissions dean once the numbers are in place? Or as Penn's Director of Admissions Eric Kaplan asks, "Amid all of those shifting currents, what do those of us who make decisions value most in a candidate? First of all, we want to see academic commitment and initiative, a rigorous scholastic record, and demonstrated excellence in nonclassroom activities." Then the question becomes, how excellent is excellent in nonclassroom activities? Let's turn to Princeton again to find out how the dean measures excellence in nonclassroom activities. The rating system for both academic and nonacademic achievement are on a scale from one to five, with one being the highest rating. Now listen to this, all of you presidents of your class, presidents of your student council, quarterbacks of your football team that led your team to the state championship: to get a one in nonacademics at Princeton (or Harvard, Yale, Columbia, and Stanford, the most selective colleges in the United States), you have to do something truly exceptional, such as making the junior Olympic team, be a founder of a start-up business about to go public, hold a patent, publish a book, act on Broadway. That's a one. That's the national or international arena of competition. Now it takes a state or regional achievement to rate a two: Eastern states tennis rating, equestrian rating, football team winning the Western division, Central states regional band, Southwestern rodeo champion, Eagle Scout leader of Florida, top clarinetist in the North-Central states. That's a two. Now a three is no slouch either! A three is tops in your own high school. If you are from a big, top academic suburban public high school, you know how much talent, time, and focus it takes to be captain of the Newton-North team, founder of Atlanta high school's gay and lesbian club, editor of Seattle's high school yearbook, president of Cleveland's Ecumenical Youth Council, first violin in the Los Angeles high school's orchestra. That's a three in Ivy competition. You will get a four in the Ivy pool if you are active (but with no particular leadership skills) in sports, belong to clubs, and play in the band, and a five with very little nonacademic achievement. Most applicants are threes. Knowing the time, loyalty, and commitment leadership roles take,

> Finding authentic seventeen year-olds with their own voice is very high on the list of top picks for deans of admissions.

you often assume that top leadership in your competitive high school will bring a much higher rating than it does. Think globally as you think of the competition for admission. After all, that's what the evaluation is—a global measure as opposed to a measure by your own teachers and school. But don't get overwhelmed by the thought. Your responsibility is to do your best within your own interests, abilities, and values. Finding authentic seventeen-year-olds with their own voice is very high on the list of top picks for deans of admissions.

CHAPTER 6

College Economics 101

How much will it really cost?

You probably don't think of winning the heart of the college admissions dean through financial aid talk, but you should know that most students get some kind of financial aid. The deans have a pot of gold from which they must bring in a freshman class that meets all of the institutional priorities. That is, each institution sets its own priorities for the makeup of its freshman class. These priorities include scholars, athletes, leadership positions, minorities, legacies, and international students. Do not believe the "hearsay" that money is not available for middle- and upper-income families. It all depends on whom the college wants in its class as well as on the number of children in your family, home mortgages, health needs of your family, and many other complex and variable factors. Check it out for yourself. Now is the time to start learning about hard ball in big-time finance. We are talking a major investment here—up to $150,000 for four years.

Paying for college used to be mostly an issue for your parents. Nowadays, given the high proportion of parents' income that college costs, you are usually the one who ends up with years of debt. Many government loans are for students, not their parents, so even though your parents may take on many of the costs of college for you, there are some things you must do yourself. Being well informed about college finances is one more way that you can show the dean of admissions that you are grown up and responsible enough to go to his selective college.

Six College Money Principles

Here are six college money principles to get you started on financial responsibility:

1. **You won't have any idea how much a college will cost until you receive your financial aid package. Convince your parents that this is true. Do not select your final list by the advertised cost of college.**

2. **You have to get your forms in on time to be competitive for the money.**

3. **College's gap. That is, even though some colleges know you can't afford to attend their college, they will still admit you, and will not offer you the financial package that you need to go there.**

4. **Negotiation with a better financial package from another college in hand is the way to go.**

5. **Don't be afraid of reasonable indebtedness.**

6. **There is a "best" financial aid Web site. It pays to check it out.**

Let's take the six college money principles from the top:

1. Cost.

Many parents hit the roof when their daughter says, "I want to go to Wellesley College, and it costs $35,000 a year." Don't take "There is no way we are paying $35,000 a year for your education when you can go to state for $15,000" for an answer! Check it out. If Wellesley is a perfect match for you, apply and fill out your financial aid forms. Then wait and see your Student Aid Reports (SAR) and how much your parents are expected to pay (Expected Family Contribution—EFC) before you start arguing. Save the fights until you can say, "Look, Mom and Pop, here are the numbers. Not what you thought, huh?" And then make your case for Wellesley. To get started on what the colleges think your parents can afford, go ahead and calculate the EFC on the Web. The College Board (www.collegeboard.org) has the easiest format to use. Throughout the college selection process, always try to keep in sight how the college is perceiving your application. A rough estimate of what your family is expected to pay gets you started on what the dean of admissions thinks it will cost the college to get you. Colleges also expect you to bring in $6,000 a year of your own. This includes a $2,000 government loan, $2,000 from a campus work-study job and summer work, and savings for the third $2,000. Therefore the college usually includes a student work-study program in your financial package, which guarantees you can earn a certain amount for the year.

2. Financial aid forms: FAFSA, PROFILE, and the colleges' own forms.

The first step in the financial aid process, even before you apply, is to check with the colleges and ask which financial aid forms they require. Free Application for Federal Student Aid (FAFSA), the federal form that everyone needs to submit, is available in November from your guidance office or online at www.fafsa.ed.gov. A helpful brochure, *The Student Guide: Financial Aid from the U.S. Department of Education,* can be requested from the same address. All lenders of federal and state money—federal Title IV student aid, Pell Grants, Stafford Loans, Supplemental Educational Opportunity Grants, College Work-Study, and the Perkins Loans—require that you complete the FAFSA. The FAFSA must be filed as close to January 1 as possible. Plan to use your parents' last year's income tax forms to estimate next year's income in order to get it in early. Don't even think of waiting until current taxes are ready before sending in your FAFSA form. No doubt about it—you won't get anywhere without the FAFSA properly filled out and sent in as close to January 1 as possible. (Don't send it before January 1, or it will be sent back and you will go to the end of the money line at most colleges.)

As many as eight hundred private, selective colleges and scholarship programs require the PROFILE form from the College Scholarship Service–CSS. You must register for the PROFILE after you know your final list of colleges. You can get the registration form in your guidance office or on the Net at www.collegeboard.org where you will find the online registration and application. Besides the PROFILE, remember that all federal and state money also require the FAFSA. Most of you will need work-study jobs, so both forms will often be required at the PROFILE colleges. Hard to believe but true, some colleges will also have their own forms in addition to the FAFSA and PROFILE. You will often need to complete the colleges' own financial aid forms to be competitive for the money. Before you give up on this deluge of forms and join the Foreign Legion instead of going to college, the good news is that they all want the same data. Once you have your parents at the kitchen table with their last year's tax records, take one form at a time and complete just the FAFSA form first. With the satisfaction of having completed the FAFSA, you will find that the other two forms are a piece of cake.

Don't even think of sending in any forms without first making several copies. Many a financial aid form gets held up or lost. In the meantime, the colleges will ask you for a copy of your FAFSA or PROFILE forms to use at the college financial aid office while they wait for the official form to arrive from the government or ETS.

3. College's gap.

It used to be that most financial aid was awarded on need. The college deans then referred to the admissions process as "need-blind admissions"—that is, they accepted or denied students without knowing their financial status. Now, with the cost of college up and soaring, most colleges can no longer afford to accept or deny without knowing the paying ability of the student.

Merit, or giving out their money according to whom they want in their college (institutional priorities) regardless of need, is the current trend for using college resources. Using their "pot of gold" for merit means that the college money is going to bring in the students that they want most: high testers to get their ratings up, high grades to get their profiles up, under-represented groups for diversity, special talented students to upgrade their orchestra or pitching team. There are so few colleges that are need-blind nowa-days that we can list them, although they can change as fast as the stock market does. Most are selective colleges with high enough endowments and few enough families of need applying that they are able to meet 100 percent of the need of their students. As of now, these schools have need-blind admissions: Amherst, Barnard, Bates, Bowdoin, Bryn Mawr, Bucknell, Colby, Colgate, Columbia, Connecticut College, Dartmouth, Denison, Georgetown, Harvard, Haverford, MIT, Middlebury, Mount Holyoke, Notre Dame, Parsons, Penn, Princeton, Reed, St. John's (MD and NM), Sarah Lawrence, Stanford, Trinity,

> **The best source for learning about your possibilities for aid is with the director of financial aid. He can be as important to you as the dean of admissions. Make a friend of the director of financial aid early in the application process. Meet him. Know his name. Get his e-mail address.**

Tufts, Union, Vassar, Wellesley, Wesleyan, Williams, and Yale. In these few colleges, admissions is not connected to your financial aid need. If accepted, these selective colleges intend to give you the necessary financial aid to attend their college.

The hard truth nowadays, though, is that most of that gold is given out for merit. So it pays for you to be aware that when merit scholarships are up, meeting the financial need of many of the applicants is down.

The best source for learning about your possibilities for aid is with the director of financial aid. He can be as important to you as the dean of admissions. Make a friend of the director of financial aid early in the application process. Meet him. Know his name. Get his e-mail address.

4. Negotiation.

Negotiating a workable financial aid package is important if you have one package that is out of line with the rest, and if you would give anything— except $50,000 indebtedness—to go to the college. Take the time to check out the possibility of getting a reevaluation of your financial need by the college. One of my students was offered $10,000 less aid from Brown where she wanted to be more than she wanted to be at the other Ivy League school that came up with the bigger package. She made an appointment with the director of financial aid at Brown a few days before May 1. When she went, she took the better package with her. She explained that Brown was where she most wanted to be, and after Brown reevaluated her case, not only did they match her package, but they came up with a few thousand more. Her family financial circumstances could be interpreted in a variety of ways, and because she was from an underrepresented group that Brown wanted on campus, she won the negotiation. Not everyone gets a match of their best package, and more often than not the bigger package comes from where you do want to go. But if the package doesn't make sense to you, take the time to visit or call the director of financial aid and give negotiation a serious try. Hey, they won't take away what you already have because you asked for more!

5. Indebtedness.

What's reasonable? Big-time college indebtedness is new since your parent's generation went to college. Nowadays the average undergraduate indebtedness at graduation is $13,788. Think about it. Have a figure in mind of how much is reasonable for you, partly depending on what career plans you have. Check out how much debt college graduates are incurring this year. If it's only $5,000, it doesn't sound like much—but that's $5,000 times four, which amounts to $20,000 in the end. On the other hand, we are talking only about the equivalent of the price of a new car. Still, if you pay that debt off in the first five years of work (when you have your lowest salary), you will have to pay $450 a month on top of rent and on top of a car payment, and that's big money!

I had a student who "had" to go to Duke until she realized the size of her indebtedness at the end of four years. Thinking it over, she realized that just getting into Duke satisfied her "prestige need," and she decided to go one year to a City University of New York school, at $3,000 a year and live at home. Abigail was so surprised that she liked it so much, that she has just completed her second year at Hunter College (CUNY) with honors and plans to take her degree there. She and her family will end up with absolutely no debt. Abigail can now afford to be a schoolteacher, her dream career, and get her master's degree on the side.

You must examine those financial packages. How much is grant or scholarship (not to be paid back)? How much is student and family contribution? How much comes from loans (to be paid back)? Count up the indebtedness for four years. Think again about your final decision of where to go in terms of four-year indebtedness.

Watch for colleges that load up on the debt; be aware of those colleges whose graduates leave with the least debt. Here are a few of the big-debt universities (with an average debt of more than $22,240): Brown, MIT, Pitzer, and Wesleyan. Four with the least amount of debt (with an average debt under $12,000) are Amherst, Beloit, Grinnell, and Rice. Indebtedness is a worthy question in April when you are deciding where to go. Be sure to ask the college rep in the fall, "What's the average debt of this year's graduates?"

6. Financial aid Web site.

The very best Web site to help you in your financial considerations is found at www.finaid.org. This Web site is sponsored by the National Association of Student Financial Aid Administrators, and there is hardly a question that can't be answered through it. Use this Web site to uncover and discover every single path that will lead to your share of the pot of gold!

Last Word on Financial Aid

After your family, the colleges are your major financial resource. Another significant resource may be your parents' employer, church, or service club. Don't waste your time and money for an extra $500 by spending 500 hours online and filling out universal applications for scholarship awards that will be deducted from what the college gives you. Get in touch with the director of financial aid as soon as you send in your application. Learn the director's name, make a friend, find out how the financial aid office can help you make your final decision on where you will go to college. Ask about the average financial package at their college, what percentage of students receive financial aid (the lower the percent, the better your chances are of getting more money), and the average graduate's indebtedness. Both *The Fiske Guide* and *The Insider's Guide* cite the percentage of students receiving financial aid in bold letters—you can't miss it!

CHAPTER 7

Final List:
Eight First Choices

You've assessed your curriculum, grades, test scores, and values. You've researched the colleges and know what they're like. You know how much your family is willing to pay for college. And now that November is here—it's final list time. November and December are the months when you must figure out to which colleges you are going to apply. First-term senior year is when you plan your strategies to win the heart of the college admissions deans in order to get the most number of choices for next April. Selecting which colleges are best for you after assessing your own ideas of what you want in a college and researching the colleges does not mean you are sure which colleges you would like best. You could always spend more time researching you and the colleges. Decisions usually must be made within a time frame. The college decision always must be made within a time frame. Now is the time when you must stop collecting data and make some decisions—ready or not.

Between your junior and senior years, you will research about twenty colleges that sound best for you, the kind of educational and campus environment where you will be happiest and most productive. You will then select a shorter list of colleges that are consistent with the *type* of college you want and that differ only in the selectivity for admissions. It makes sense to apply only to colleges where you have a reasonable chance for admission.

This is not the time when you are choosing where you are going to go to college. Don't get into some false fights at home at final list time about where you are going or not going to go. Wait until you hear from the colleges. Many seniors ruin their last year at home fighting about whether they will go to Rice or Cal Tech, and in April they learn that they didn't get into either college, wasting all of that family life that could have been wonderful for everyone in the senior year. Fall is the time that you set up your options, in order to get choices in April—or a decision in December if you are applying early. Let's say you have at least ten or twelve colleges in mind for your final eight. You will soon realize, as all scientists do who collect data, that your research is never complete. Anthropologists know that there is always more to learn about a culture. You will keep learning more and more about yourself and your colleges until May 1 when you send in your deposit for a place in the freshman class. But by November or December of your senior year, you must narrow your final college list to your final eight (or five or six or ten).

Do You Want to Get In?

As you look at your list of twenty colleges, the first question to ask yourself is not, "Can I get in?" but "Do I want to get in?" What have you learned about this campus culture? Is this the environment where you will be happiest and most productive? The next question is, "Can I get in?" What are your chances of getting in with your numbers, from your high school? How can you be sure you have two or three options next April? You can't go by the general guidelines of grades and SATs listed in the guidebooks. Those numbers are "in general," from "average" high schools. The college admissions deans know the different high schools. They will take only As from some high schools, and dip to Bs and Cs at others because they know that the competition varies from school to school. The deans accept a great range of SAT and ACT scores. Remember that no test score will get you in. Remember too, that a 650–650 won't keep you out of anywhere. The counselor or teacher who helps students in your high school with the college process has to help you with the question of where you can get in. That means figuring out the chances of admission for eight colleges, knowing who gets in which colleges from the past two or three years with *your* numbers, from *your* high school. You will want to balance your list in terms of selectivity for admission, not balance between big and small, East and West, urban and rural. Your final eight should be all the things you value most, and the main difference between them is only the selectivity for admission.

Balancing your final list requires experience and information. A critical strategy to keep your mind open in the process is not to use emotionally loaded labels for the colleges on your list. You should know that no one gets to go to a "dream school" and nobody wants to go to a "safety school." You'll never hear a senior in May proudly saying, "I'm going to my safety." Let's agree to use numbers instead of labels to describe that final list. Numbers, percentages, or odds are determined by the college decisions made for your particular high school in past years. Your guidance counselor can make an educated guess, using the statistics of your graduating class for the past two or three years. Your list should include one or two colleges where you have a 25 percent chance to get in; two or three with a 50 percent chance; one or two 75 percents; and one or two 90 percent chances to get in—all places you want to go. No one needs a college on his final list just because he can get in. If you can't think of eight places you want to go, go back to the guidebooks and research the colleges until you do. You've got over 2,400 four-year accredited colleges to choose from and three hundred of the top 10 percent colleges to search for in *Fiske* and *Insider's*!

When you figure out your numbers, you will often ask, "Aren't I allowed just one dream school?" while actually thinking, "I'll beat the odds. I'll make Chicago, Pomona, the University of Virginia. I'll be sorry all of my life if I don't give it a try." At the same time, your counselor knows that the dream school is pure fantasy, out of the ballpark. We are not talking here about a 10 percent chance to get into a so-called "reach" college. We are not talking here about a legacy, a development case, a minority student, an international student with money, a major athlete, or the first violin from the Cincinnati orchestra either. We are talking here about the second quintile, solid B student in a very competitive, suburban high school, with two or three APs, a 600 verbal and 650 math who has all-state sports, who was class president, and who performed top-of-the-line community service—and who doesn't have a prayer for Harvard, Princeton, and Stanford. Not a prayer. Or the same student with calculus or AP foreign languages who won't hold up for the first cut at Cornell, Wesleyan, Northwestern, or the University of Texas. We may also be talking about the nicest kid in the world—the one who overcame the overcomable obstacles of learning disabilities, a sister in a bulimic institute, a brother kicked out of prep school for drinking, the favorite of the whole faculty.

What is wrong with one or two dream schools on the final list? Here is what is wrong. A dream school is a definite deny to the counselor but not to the student. The student and his parents only appease the counselor and say that they will be sure to learn about other colleges. But, in the end, they learn only more about Dream U. So, when college talk comes up at home, in the car, at the mall, at Thanksgiving dinner, at the cocktail party, "She is applying to Stanford" silences all future conversation about the other colleges. "We have to get in our Stanford application" is all that sinks in.

The real danger is that you will never get engaged in learning about the other colleges on your list. Duke's Director of Admissions Christoph Guttentag agrees. He tells me that he can't count the numbers of times that denied students and their parents say to him, "I applied to other schools, but I never thought I'd have to go to them. I only want to come to Duke."

"If only those students had researched the other colleges on their list, if only they had become excited about all of their college list, they wouldn't be as let down when two or three of the denials come rolling in," cautions Guttentag.

Let's say that Davidson is on your list and yet your curriculum and grades don't stand up to Davidson's competition for admission. Even though you have the facts in front of you, you keep learning more and more about Davidson. You spend your senior year thinking you "have" to get into your dream school, even if you act cool about it to your counselor who suggests you research some less competitive colleges. Every college visit is back to Davidson. You compare all the other colleges on your list to the one that you will never be able to attend. You keep comparing those other top colleges on your final list—Rhodes, Rollins, and Richmond—by your view of Davidson. You judge rather than collect data. You jump to the conclusion of your independent study in decision making without regard to the evidence. You will always come up disappointed in April because in November you closed your mind to the terrific possibilities you have with your academic record and values. The goal of this final list is to yield two or three college choices where you really want to go. You are playing hard ball here, and you want each pitch to count. Don't throw away the few pitches in the strike zone because you don't like the sound of the name!

> **The goal of this final list is to yield two or three college choices where you really want to go.**

As you prepare your final list of eight colleges it is hard to realize that colleges are more than their competitive level for admission. Because Middlebury is harder to get into than Connecticut College, Macalester, and Colorado College doesn't make Middlebury better! If you go to Colorado College, chances are very high that by Christmas time of your freshman year you will wonder what ever possessed you to think that Middlebury was the one and only place for you. Because it's easier to get into the University of Oregon and Ohio State than it is to get into Berkeley and the University of Virginia doesn't mean that smart kids aren't challenged there. After all, a university is composed of many colleges, each with varying admission standards. The popularity of a university often inflates the competition for admission. This is the pure economics of supply and demand. It has nothing to do with being better—better means numbers in freshman classes, access to professors and to the courses you want, quality of campus housing, quality of life outside the classroom, numbers of students going on to graduate schools or graduating with jobs in outstanding training programs. Think of colleges as stock. Why invest in an overvalued college? Usually overvalued means you've heard a lot about it, and its name is on the tip of everyone's tongue. Why? Often because of its football and basketball teams—it may have nothing to do with academics.

Eight First Choices: The Final Eight

Let's be clear on the goal for your final list. You are *not* choosing, now, where you will go. You are after the greatest number of college options possible in April. Looking at your list as the options you want next April frees you to get to know a lot more about all of those colleges on your list. You will like best what you know best. If an older brother is at Johns Hopkins, that's best. If you went to soccer camp at Skidmore, that's best. If your favorite college team is Duke or Notre Dame, they're the best! Don't learn more and more about one or two colleges and think that you "have" to go to Sewanee or Wake Forest. Get to know best all eight colleges on your final list.

You will like best what you know best. Get to know best all eight colleges on your final list.

In order to get to know best all of the colleges on your list, try very hard *not* to prioritize your final list. If you think, "I have eight first choices," rather than a first, second, fifth, and eighth choice, you will put enthusiastic energy and thoughtful responses into all of your applications and essays. Many seniors have been shocked that they didn't get into what they considered the fourth, fifth, seventh, or eighth college on their list. Later they learned that the college found their application sloppy and that it showed little interest in the college. This "don't prioritize" strategy will keep you writing meaningful applications with distinguishing short answers on all eight of the colleges on your final list. You will respond with equal enthusiasm to six to eight college reps when they visit your high school this fall.

Loving all eight colleges and letting the deans of admissions know of your high interest in each of them is the secret for creating the most number of April options in your senior year. You'll be smiling in April when those fat letters come rolling in. You'll know you've won the hearts of several college admisisons deans. And if you manage to keep your mind open and to keep collecting the data after April, even after those acceptances come in, many of you will be surprised at what your final decision will be.

> Loving all eight colleges and letting the deans of admissions know of your high interest in each of them is the secret for creating the most number of April options in your senior year.

April 15: *Now* is the time to argue with your parents. You know the college decisions. You know what you want from a college, and you know your college cultures. April 15 until May 1 is when you build a strong case for yourself about deciding where you will go next year. The power is *all* yours.

One First Choice: Early Decision, Early Action

Flying in the face of "eight first choices" are the colleges' early plans. Don't even think about early decision until you have finalized your college list. Let's face it, early decision is great for the colleges. They lock in top testers who can pay the full cost early in the year. When they talk to you, you would almost think it was to your advantage to go early. But whoa! Let's look at the downside to an early plan. I know. I know. You are going to ask, "What have I got to lose?" The college reps are out there hustling for as many applications as they can bring in. Here is another point of view for you to consider, from the applicant side of the fence. Besides the obvious things about early decision that hurt the student (a deferral or denial in December just before exams, being unable to learn more about the college match, basing your college admissions on your junior year and not waiting for senior grades and stronger SATs)—everyone has to admit that it cuts decision time in half. The student has to know by October where he is applying and have the application in by November 1 or 15. The unqualified students for early decision (those who don't have the numbers to get in) have the impression that they will get in because of their high interest. "If we are really your first choice, then apply early!" is the clear message from most of the college admissions officers. This is said in information sessions without having a clue about the particular student's academic record. The worst part of early plans, however, isn't all the above disadvantages. The worst part of eary plans is that early applications close minds. The student's primary task is to research the colleges to learn what's out there, to see the differences in campus cultures, to keep taking in data as an anthropologist or any scientist does in research. Students learn in science class that they must keep collecting data and evaluate only after all the data are in. This is no place for early judgment or guessing a hypothesis ("I don't like this, I love that") before the data are in.

Let me tell you what happens to the research component in early decision: A senior will write to me in the summer and say, "I love Dartmouth, I'm going to apply early, I had an interview and it went on for an hour and twenty minutes." This student doesn't have the numbers to get into Dartmouth. I write back and say, "Bob, I know you love Dartmouth. Now let's go on and see what else you like. What is it you like about Dartmouth? Here is a list of colleges just like it, with varying degrees of selectivity to get you started." All of that goes in one ear and out the other because the student (and this is very typical) only has eyes for Dartmouth. So he keeps learning more and more about one college. And we all like best what we know best. When the student is denied or deferred in late December, not only can he not think straight because he is so disappointed and surprised (regardless of how cool he may handle it), he just can't begin to open his mind at that late date. Some go through the motions, but they don't get engaged in learning more about several other colleges.

Your responsibility is to figure out what you really like. Your responsibility is to come up with eight *first* choices. No one gets to know best their sixth, seventh, and eighth choice if they prioritize before they know their options—that is, which colleges have admitted them and which have not. Those who have late decisions to make (that is, those who have been placed on wait lists), often change their minds as to where they want to go because they have had the time to collect the data for several colleges. That's because they have been learning about the colleges with an open mind, and their parents have almost always given them permission to do so (that is, the parents didn't get stuck on their child's early choice).

> Early decision closes minds. A closed mind is the worst way to make a decision. It drastically shuts out the best possibilities for higher education. Learning how to make sound decisions is a major by-product of the college selection process.

So there you have it. Early decision closes minds. A closed mind is the worst way to make a decision. It drastically shuts out the best possibilities for higher education. Learning how to make sound decisions is a major by-product of the college selection process.

Early decision is a strategy that usually helps the colleges a lot more than it helps students because early plans reduce your decision-making time by half. Getting the process "over with" doesn't begin to outweigh the advantages that learning more about the colleges and yourself during your senior year will bring you. If you have a 10 to 25 percent chance of getting in, and it's a competitive college on the national scene, don't buy in to the colleges' message to "Apply early if you clearly like it best." What harm will it do? Getting a deferral or a denial at exam time in December, with no acceptances to balance the denial, hurts. And it hurts a lot more in December than you think it will in September. And just as important, a very small percentage of those deferred students ever get in from the regular pool (10 to 15 percent). Think about it. Plain human behavior. If you read through an applicant's folder that you had turned down the first time, wouldn't you say to yourself, "Well, I didn't take her in the first round, wouldn't I rather say yes to a fresh, new applicant than the one I denied earlier? "Of course you would! We all would. Even though the colleges want to lock in the high flyers (top testers), and the media touts the national trend toward earlies, it is never to your advantage unless you have what that college is looking for—the numbers. Of course I'll agree that there are always exceptions. It probably makes sense for about 10 percent of your class to apply early for one reason or another. If one of the colleges in your "50 percent chances to get in" stands out in high interest for you, or if financial aid or minority status is not a factor in your admissions, then it might make sense for you to consider applying early. The colleges talk to you only about your interest, but the colleges act on your interest *only* if you have their numbers. If you aren't quite up there, don't even think of applying early. On the other hand, if you do have the numbers, you have researched your whole list, and you have considered the data you collect-ed as an anthropologist would (rather than judging by hearsay and reputa-tion), then early plans can give you a competitive edge over regular applicants because the college is assured that you will accept their offer.

PART II

Applying to College

CHAPTER 8

College Essay

When it comes time to write your college applications, you will see that the only thing that holds you back from completing them is your essay. Most of the application can be written in short spurts of time, between homework and school activities. The essay, however, takes a major amount of time, with many drafts to get it as well done as it needs to be. Once you have the numbers to get in, the essay is probably *the* most important part of your application. Let's keep in mind that the Ivy deans are the first to admit that they turn away as many qualified and fascinating students as the students they take. That's where the essay comes in. If you've got the numbers that won't keep you out (please notice, all of you SAT buffs, numbers never get you in), there is one criterion above all others that makes a difference and tips the admissions committee toward a student. The single criterion is the ability to write—writing as demonstrated in your college essay and in your classroom written papers. John E. Hanson, Director of Admissions at Middlebury College, likes to see the various drafts of senior classroom papers with teacher comments before he decides on the writing ability of the student. He and his staff take the time to look at what level of instruction you are getting in your high school, and they judge by what you have learned from the opportunities you have been given.

Who Are You?

Your essay is a natural place to distinguish yourself from your classmates. Often it is read before the transcript is read, and the "you" of your essay is in the mind of the dean as he looks at your grades and the level of challenge you chose for your high school curriculum. Think carefully about the questions asked of you and spend the necessary time to formulate your response. This is your opportunity to communicate to the admissions committee who the person behind those numbers is—the real you. Just think, this is probably the only document for which the college admissions dean doesn't have a particular expectation. It is the only component of your college file that isn't already on your record. It is the part of your application where you can start from scratch today and make something special of yourself—just as you have in your academics for the past twelve years.

> Your essay is a natural place to distinguish yourself from your classmates. This is your opportunity to communicate to the admissions committee who the person behind those numbers is—the real you.

Writing the Essay

Your college essay is your best opportunity to distinguish yourself from other applicants. You have a chance to show your ability to think and write, and also what your character, values, beliefs, and aspirations are. It doesn't matter what your topic is, although the essay should not be a description of events. Here is what Harvard's Dean of Admissions William R. Fitzsimmons is looking for in your essay: the quality of your thinking, your questioning nature, your openness to ideas, and your unique way of expressing your ideas. And if Bill Fitzsimmons is looking for those qualities in your essay, you can be sure you are on the right essay track with all of the college deans by listening to his measure of the essay. Your college essay must be a lot more than a description of an event or activity, it must be an essay about what you've learned from the experience. No matter how technically correct your essay is, it's your creative intelligence that the college is trying to measure. After all, they have your English grades and test scores, so they know where you stand in being able to put your thoughts together. "It's the thoughts that you have, your unique way of putting ideas and events together, learning from literature, and your life of the mind that will distinguish you in the selective applicant pool," advises Harvard's Fitzsimmons.

Make the transition from writing assignments in English class to a personal style for your college essay. I read hundreds of senior's first drafts, and all too often respond with, "Mr. English Teacher will love this. It's really well written, but I can't tell who you are. It's too generic teenage, 'everything will come out all right if only I try harder.' What about your struggle with geometry, your disappointment in your test scores, your breakup with your boyfriend, your love of French literature—now those are *your* things. Who are you, anyway, with all of those things going on? No one else in the applicant pool is going to have your take on your issues!"

Once the draft is written, you know your perception of your essay. Now switch over and think how the college admissions dean is looking at your essay. You can't win the dean's heart if you don't know what he values! Always figure out your own perceptions of what you are doing in the process: on the application, at the interview, at the college fair, on your essay, and then switch your mind over to the perception and point of view of the college dean before you act. Read on. . . .

What Deans of Admissions Look For

Let's hear it from one Duke admissions officer—what she has to say about essays from her side of the desk and what she wants out of students. Rachel Toor, former admissions officer at Duke, wrote about current college essays in the *Chronicle of Higher Education* (June 2, 2000), the first and last daily word on college news. She says that *The Catcher in the Rye* is still the number one book that seniors write about, with *The Great Gatsby* coming in second. There are a lot of cultural identity Asian kids reading and writing about *The Joy Luck Club,* Jewish kids about *The Chosen* or *Night,* and Asian Indians writing about *Siddhartha.* And then, says Toor, there are all of those white kids writing gee-whiz essays about *Invisible Man* and the Toni Morrison books. *Into Thin Air* is a hit for an essay book, as are *A Prayer for Owen Meany, The Things They Carried, Cold Mountain,* and *Memoirs of a Geisha.* "No surprises here," says Toor. Most of the article, however, was about Toor's astonishment and disappointment with the frequent citing of *Tuesdays with Morrie.* Her disappointment is that it is such a safe book. It's a motherhood and apple-pie book—all about love, friendship, long walks—nothing risky. This brings her article to the big question: "How come seventeen-year-olds never talk about sex? Why can't they find a way to write about gender and sexuality?" Toor concludes her lament with "I guess these kids will continue to read about *Tuesdays with Morrie.* And we'll continue to read what they think about it." Now seniors. Let that be a lesson to you. Don't write about *Tuesdays with Morrie!* And just think how unique you'd be if you dared write about relationships and gender. While we're with the perceptions of the former Duke admissions officer, let's go right on and look at how a typical college admissions dean is looking at *your* essay.

Picture this: It's 6:55 P.M., dark and raining. A half-cup of cold coffee sits on the floor leaning against a stack of essays. The dean has just finished reading seventy-eight college essays in one day, which she has tossed in another stack. She is late for her seven o'clock Friday night date. As she urges herself, "Read just one more before you go," she hastily grabs your essay.

If it's about environment, community service, or your favorite teacher, she groans before she even notices who wrote it. If your essay's theme is one of the 3 Ds (divorce, depression, or drugs), she is in agony. If that "just one more before I go" essay is about a sitcom on TV or *Tuesdays with Morrie,* watch out! If your essay is about God, love, injustice, death, or the purpose of life, it had better be funny! So. Before you even get started on your college essay, give some serious thought to what's trendy and shy as far away as you can from it. No matter how unsure you are, try to trust your own idea of what to write about.

A Reflection of You

Making the most of the essay opportunity is a reflection of how you are able to make the most of any advantage or opportunity that comes your way. Making the most of the essay shows how you have learned to handle other opportunities in high school. It can also provide an expression of your attitudes and your understanding of the campus environment where you want to go.

You have a chance to express the you that you know best and are most proud of. It doesn't matter what the question is or what your topic is. All the colleges want to know the same thing. What does this seventeen-year-old think? What has she learned about herself and the world given the opportunities she has had in life? What kinds of learning attitudes and intellectual curiosity does he have? How confident is she? How together, for a seventeen-year-old, is he? The answer to these questions can come from any topic. More than a description of events, your college essay must tell how you feel about the event or activity, and what you've learned from the experience. In other words, if you write about your dad, or grandmother, or a bike trip through China that you took last summer, or a community service job you held in Chile—no matter how dramatic—tell about the person or event in a short paragraph and use the rest of the essay to tell what you learned from the person or experience, or how you've changed

Be yourself and go with the essay that has the most "you" in it, not necessarily the most academic or politically correct essay. Trust me. No—better yet, trust you!

because of it. Write about what you have learned about you, the world, and other people. No matter what the question—who or what has influenced you the most—the task is not to write about the "who" or the "what." The college admissions dean wants to know what fascinates you about the "who" or the "what." Your college essay documents how you stand out from your pals and all those other seniors applying to Selective U!

Writing and Content Tips for Your College Essay

▶ Write several drafts before the essay is final.

▶ Use all the standard rules of good writing. Be concise, be interesting, and use a "grabber" in the first line or paragraph to catch the attention of the readers. Remember: The readers will read thousands of high school senior essays.

▶ Use a font big enough for the admissions staff to easily read.

▶ Shorten the essay—not the spaces between the lines—to fit the essay into the required space! Most seniors have a hard time cutting their essays; ask your English teacher to help you with that part.

▶ Many of you will want help with your essay. See your English teacher and your guidance counselor for both creative and technical help—that is, content ideas and correct grammar and spelling.

▶ Don't try to write what you think the committee wants to hear. Readers are not looking for something in particular; they are looking to learn more about who you are.

▶ The topic doesn't have to be dramatic or bizarre or unusual. You can write about the most ordinary daily activity you do or a story you read. It's what you learn and observe or how you've changed that counts.

▶ Never use the essay to tell why you have such poor grades, or how you know your next term will be better. An essay of excuses, no matter how valid, highlights your weaknesses. Your essay should always lead from your strengths. If you feel you have a good reason for poor grades, discuss it with your guidance counselor; she's the one to tell the colleges the excuses, not you.

▶ The more selective the college, the more emphasis it usually places on the essay. Good colleges expect good writers.

▶ Most importantly, remember that English isn't just for English class! Apply the good writing skills you have learned in class. Make the transition from writing assignments in class to the writing of your essay. Tie in a literary reference, a character or event that you've read about. Integrating your personal statement with literature can be an interesting way to write a college essay.

What's it going to be? The written word of a very interesting young person who is excited about going away to college next year. If your teacher or counselor says it won't do (not up to your rigorous curriculum and grades), be quick to write another. Be prepared to rewrite a half dozen times. Technically correct won't make it; remember you may be the seventy-ninth applicant's essay read in that long, dreary day. I know that you aren't boring. It's just that when teens get scared or anxious they often write as if they are. You will want to send in a college essay that measures up to who you really are. Be yourself and go with the essay that has the most "you" in it, not necessarily the most academic or politically correct essay. Trust me. No—better yet, trust you!

CHAPTER 9

The Application

The first written communication to the dean of college admissions will be your application. It is filed first—on top of everything else in your folder—and as far as the dean is concerned that application *is* you. So be sure it looks as good as you get—spelling- and grammar-wise, neatness too! Writing your application is a major opportunity to distinguish yourself—to document your clarity, creativity, and competence. Let me tell you why. Everyone will tell you that the college essay is crucial to win the heart of the college admissions dean. That's true—but everyone knows it. What many are not aware of is that your college applications can be as creative as your essay. College admissions deans read thousands of applications, so yours has to stand out—just like *you* do! I don't mean stand out in a quirky, gimmicky way but in a "who you are" way. The application strategy that I teach my students is to write not what the college can do for you (provide you with a strong biology program because you, like everyone else, want to go to medical school), write what you can do for the college. The dean is looking for a strong freshman community that every high school senior in the world will want to be a part of. He wants a class that provides the college with high energy leadership in intellectual curiosity, publications, music, student government, athletics, creative thinking, and the arts.

> **The dean is looking for a strong freshman community that every high school senior in the world will want to be a part of. He wants a class that provides the college with high energy leadership in intellectual curiosity, publications, music, student government, athletics, creative thinking, and the arts.**

The dean is reading your application to evaluate if you are going to be a good match for his college and provide his community with any of those leadership categories he is seeking. If you have a high school record of integrating black and white students on the state or regional level, highlight it. The dean is checking to figure out how well you can handle freedom. If you are a political activist against drinking, say so! Colleges know they need as many aggressive nondrinkers as they can get. Let's take a closer look at the steps you must take in preparing your eight applications that hopefully will win four deans' hearts.

Organizing Applications

Try to get all of your college applications in hand by October of your senior year. It often takes three weeks to receive an application by mail, so request them as soon as you know your final list. Better yet, download each application from the homepage of the college on the Web, or get all of your applications from one site—either www.collegedge.com, one of the first companies to offer the quick and easy way out of acquiring applications, or *Princeton Review*'s Apply! at www.weapply.com.

Now is the time to organize. Organize beyond organize. It must be "Hello, control! Good-bye, chaos!" for you. Throw away all of those brochures, view books, letters, and applications in your room and under your bed that are not on your final list. Just go right ahead, throw them out! You don't need the clutter. You have made your decisions; you know your final list.

You've done your research, collected your data, and you're right: The final list is perfect for you. Throw away the others you were considering! Go to the business supplies section of a store, find a business office supplies catalog, or get on the Web and buy nine expanding folders—one for each of the eight colleges on your final list and the other for your "central office." In your central office folder, you will keep a list of your final eight, and every requirement and deadline each of them expects you to meet: their test requirements, application deadlines, and financial aid forms required. On that deadline list, include the Secondary School Report (SSR), essays, interview, and teacher recommendations that each college requires. On the following pages is a sample College Application Organizer designed by one of my seniors that, I think you will agree, is a perfect example of "organize beyond organize." Some of you will want to copy it to keep track of Part I and Part II of your application deadlines. Others of you will get the idea by just looking at it. It's a great organizational model however you decide to use it. Your central office folder is the perfect place to put all of your SAT or ACT numbers: your registration number found on the blue student copy, your high school CEEB code, and the college codes. Everything. Right after the forms required, with deadlines, write down the name of the person responsible for sending the forms to the college: with the name of someone in your guidance office for sending the SSR and transcript; your teachers for sending the teacher recommendations; and you for sending test and financial aid forms and scores. Keep all of your correspondence and copies of your e-mails to the college dean in its proper folder. Add your research notes to each college folder.

You will organize in the fall, as soon as you determine your final list—long before you panic and can't think straight. This way you'll avoid having your parents on your back beyond belief asking you what is due and have you sent it in, and why haven't you. At that time of year—right around Thanksgiving—you'll do well to remember your final list. This organization idea is really family damage control. You will learn a very important lesson here—God blesses all of the organizers of college applications (even if this is the only time in your life when you are so well organized). Just you wait and see.

College Application Organizer

		College #1 Bates	College #2 Denison	College #3 Grinnell
College Name				
College Representative		W. Mitchell	P. Robinson	J. Sumner
E-mail		Admissions@bates.edu	Admissions@denison.edu	Askgrin@grinnell.edu
Address		23 Campus Ave., Lewiston, ME 04240	Box H, Granville, OH 43023	PO Box 805, Grinnell, IA 50112
Part I (or Common Application Supplement)	Due Date	ASAP	ASAP	ASAP
	Supplemental Essay (if any)	0	0	0
	Done	✓	✓	✓
	Xeroxed	✓	✓	✓
	Check/fee waiver	$50	$40	$30
	Sent	12/1	12/1	12/1
Teacher Recommend-ations	Ms. Schutt	11/12	11/12	11/12
	Mr. Fernandez	11/12	11/12	11/12
Secondary School Report (SSR)		11/12	11/12	11/12
Midyear Report				
Part II	Due Date	2/1	2/1	1/20
	Essay #1	1/1	1/1	1/3
	Essay #2 (if any)	1/15	1/15	1/3
	Done	✓	✓	✓
	Checked (by you AND someone else)	Mr. Loughery	Mr. Loughery	Ms. Schutt
	Xeroxed	✓	✓	✓
	Postcard	✓	✓	✓
	Check/fee waiver (if there was no Part I)	✓	✓	✓
	Sent	1/25	1/25	1/12
Interview	Date	10/8	Alum 2/8	Alum 1/28
	Interviewer	C. McCoy	A. Reed	NYC: J. Pei
	Thank you note	✓	✓	✓
College Testing Requirements (SAT I, SAT II, ACT, TOEFL, etc.)		ACT; SAT; SAT II optional; TOEFL required for international	ACT or SAT I; TOEFL for international	ACT or SAT I; TOEFL for international
Extra Materials (tapes, art, additional recommendations, etc.)		2/14	2/14	2/14
Application complete & sent		1/25	1/25	1/12

College #4 Haverford	College #5 Macalester	College #6 Middlebury	College #7 Pitzer	College #8 Wesleyan
D. Phillips	L. Robinson	J. Hanson	Rodriguez	C. Thornton
Admitme@haverford.edu	Admissions@mac-alester.edu	Admissions@middle-bury.edu	Admissions@pit-zer.edu	Admission@wes-leyan.edu
370 Lancaster Ave.,Haverford, PA 19041	1600 Grand Ave., St. Paul, MN 55105	131 So. Main, Middlebury, VT 05753	1050 N. Mills Ave., Claremont, CA 91711	70 Wyllis Ave., Middletown, CT 06459
ASAP	ASAP	ASAP	ASAP	ASAP
✓	0	✓	0	0
✓	✓	✓	✓	✓
✓	✓	✓	✓	✓
$50	$40	$55	$40	$55
12/10	12/10	12/1	12/10	12/10
11/20	11/20	11/12	11/20	11/20
11/20	11/20	11/12	11/20	11/20
11/20	11/20	11/12	11/20	11/20
1/15	1/13	12/15	2/1	1/1
1/3	1/3	12/1	1/1	12/1
1/3	1/3	12/1	1/15	12/1
✓	✓	✓	✓	✓
Mrs. Wien	Mrs. Wien	Ms. Schutt	Mr. Loughery	Ms. Schutt
✓	✓	✓	✓	✓
✓	✓	✓	✓	✓
✓	✓	✓	✓	✓
✓	✓	✓	✓	✓
10/20	11/15 school	10/9	2/6 alum	10/18
campus student	L. Robinson	C. Perine On campus	J. Larskin	Information session
✓	✓	✓	✓	✓
ACT or SAT I; 3 SAT II incl. Writing	ACT or SAT I; SAT II optional; TOEFL or ELIOT for international	ACT or 3 SAT II; TOEFL for international	ACT or SAT I; 3 SAT II incl. Writing, Math recommended	ACT or SAT I; 3 SAT II incl. Writing
2/14	2/14	2/14	2/14	2/14
1/8	1/8	12/7	1/25	12/23

Designed by Caroline Wekselbaum

The Common Application

The Common Application can be used for over two hundred colleges. Most selective colleges, however, measure your interest in their college in many ways—using their own application is one of them. There is a psychological edge when you use the particular college's special application. You can't win the heart of the college admissions dean if you send out twenty common apps, each college reading like the other. Using the college's own application (some of them have only the Common Application with a supplementary form) indicates that you are interested enough to write to their specific college rather than applying to as many as you can with a single form—lottery style. If you do use the Common Application, make certain that you save the original and that the copies are clear and readable.

Number of Applications

If your list is mostly to the top 10 percent of America's most selective colleges, you should plan to apply to no less than eight colleges, with a range of competition for admission.

Read chapter 7—Final List, and plan to choose two colleges in each category: schools where you have a 25 percent chance, 50 percent chance, 75 percent chance, and 90 percent chance to get in. Some students choose four 50 percents and no 25 percents. Others choose three 50s and three 75s, and two 90s. As long as you have at least two 75s and two 90s on your list, I don't care how you distribute the 25s and 50s. When you are figuring out your competitive standing to get in, keep in mind that the colleges and demographics tell us that each year until 2008 is going to be more competitive. Make sure that you are telling yourself the truth about your 90 percent chances to get in colleges on your final list. Try to evaluate your academic record as clearly as you can. It's hard to do, because so many seniors think that "my senior grades are going to be better" is going to happen or that hope and prayer will get them in. The dean of admissions doesn't see it that way, he goes by what your record is, not on what you hope for. Students with a B/C average and 600 SAT verbal and math scores will not have a reasonable chance at the highly competitive colleges. On the other side of the coin, don't apply to any college where you don't want to go. There is no sense in applying to University State College because it takes "everybody" and you want a place where you know you will get in if, in fact, you would never go there! I just can't begin to tell you how many seniors come to me in tears in April to say, "State College is the only place I got in, and I never wanted to go there." It's too late. You can't go back in April and research the colleges and get your application in by the January or February deadlines. You are working toward finding colleges that are consistent with your ideal college and have a range of selectivity for admissions. As Duke's Director of Admissions Christoph Guttentag cautions, "Be sure you choose your 90s *within* your ideal campus cultures."

Writing the Application

When you look at the various applications that you have to complete, you're likely to think that it looks time consuming and very boring to fill in all of those questions over and over again. It certainly doesn't look like the document that is going to win anyone's heart—and that's my point! Here's your chance to get an edge on those thousands of dull applications that all look alike and that the deans fall asleep reading. And here's how: You are going to be creative with that boring application. You are going to color outside the lines. There are a lot of places on an application where you can distinguish yourself. One rule is not to leave anything blank. It asks for academic honors and you don't have any? How about AP courses? If nothing else, fill in that you have to meet academic requirements to take the AP courses in your school (if you do, that is!). How about those Latin exams in ninth grade? If you really can't come up with anything,

> You are working toward finding colleges that are consistent with your ideal college and have a range of selectivity for admissions.

either draw a little line in the space, so the dean knows you saw the question, or better yet, write a phrase about how competitive your high school is, or some academic achievement that your school isn't formally calling an honor.

> **You are going to be creative with that boring application. You are going to color outside the lines. There are a lot of places on an application where you can distinguish yourself.**

The activities section gives you a lot of latitude for distinguishing yourself. Don't bother with a lot of ninth grade activities that you have since dropped. Rice's Richard Stabell points out to applicants that the colleges are looking for long-term commitment to two or three activities. The question the college is trying to get at here is how you spend your time outside of classroom work. The dean wants to know about your leadership and involvement, and how much time you spend in that activity. Take the time to figure it out. American college deans are always trying to measure character. Looking at how you spend your time and what you value gives them their measure of you. If you have a passion for dance and choreography, rather than fill in all the columns as found on the application, use that space to do your own thing: Write a few sentences describing your time and leadership in dance. When you are writing about your activities, think about what message you are giving. You're good? How good? You run? How fast? You play? What level of music do you play? You act? What plays were you in, what were your roles? How much time did you spend in sports, on publications, in the performing arts? Specifics are what you are after. Which position do you play and how good is the team? How many goals did you score? You write? Where were you published? Has your school paper or yearbook won any national awards? *Specificity* is what's needed to show how you stand out from all the other qualified applicants. Specifics are key for your college rep to get a clear and complete picture of who you are. You won't win a heart without being specific.

Don't forget to include your paid jobs and unpaid home responsibilities.

Harvard's Dean of Admissions Bill Fitzsimmons tells about a student from rural New England who didn't mention that he had to work on the family farm after school and every weekend because he thought, "A big shot college dean wouldn't want to know about ordinary labor." Wrong! Whether you are running the school newspaper, caring for younger siblings at home, food shopping for the family, or selling clothes at the Gap, the colleges want to know how you spend your time.

Use the application to write what you are crazy about, and something you haven't written about in your essay. In other words, use the application questions as guidelines, not as rigid categories where you have to put exactly what they ask for.

Short Answers Call for Creativity

Besides the essay, the application often includes questions asking for one paragraph or shorter answers. Most students slide over these, but here's another opportunity for you to get the edge and to win a heart. The question, "Why are you applying to Bard? or Evergreen? or UC Santa Cruz?" is after how well you know the college, how well you did your research. As an anthropologist who has been collecting data on this campus culture, you will do very well on this question! Sometimes the short-answer question is "What do you expect your major will be?" "What career are you headed for?" *Never* say or check undecided, and *never* write or check that you don't know. "Wait. What if I am undecided and I don't know?" Well, of course, most of you are undecided or don't know, but you don't want to miss this opportunity to tell more about yourself. You are trying to give the dean of admissions real insight into who you are. Let's say you don't have a clue about your major. In that case say something along that line that you *do* know. For example, "I don't know where it will take me, but right now AP Latin is by far my favorite subject and the one I most enjoy studying." Or, "Everyone in my family says I should be a doctor because I love biology and chemistry, but all I know is that I want to keep learning more science; I don't know which science I'll like

> **Never say or check undecided, and never write or check that you don't know.**

best in college." Or, "As much as I like the academics, I have to say that it's music that interests me most right now. I don't want to go to a music college or conservatory, but I do want to be sure there are plenty of music opportunities for me at college." See what I mean? Doesn't that make sense? The dean learns a lot more about you from what you do know about yourself than he would learn if you checked the undecided (lost opportunity) box.

In summary, the application is an opportunity for you to shine and to establish who you are, what you value, how you spend your time, what kinds of academics you like best, and how well you can express yourself in a small space. Many students miss out on this chance to distinguish themselves. If you put it right up there with the importance of the essay, you'll surely win the heart of the admissions dean who dreads reading most of the very ordinary applications that seniors manage to send in. Wake up those deans and admissions reps. They will love reading a creative application for a change. Get your own voice and personality into the application, as well as into your essay.

Photocopy your blank application before you make a mark on it. Don't even think of making less than three photocopies of each application. No kidding—some students go through twelve attempts before they are satisfied that it looks right. Hide the original application deep in your folder until you're sure you've got it how you want it. If the worst of the worst happens and you mess up the original, don't worry; the deans are perfectly happy with the clear photocopy you've made of the original.

Supplementary Materials

The college application consists of the points that you fill in plus the materials that you ask others to send in. Test scores, secondary school reports, and letters of recommendation are all supplementary materials that you are responsible for getting to the dean. Take a look at the best way to go about this responsibility.

Reporting Test Scores to Colleges

You are responsible for releasing your Score Choice scores and for having your *official* test scores sent from ETS in Princeton to your colleges. If you have not listed your colleges on your SAT or ACT registration forms (the scores will be sent to four colleges that you designate at no extra charge), then you must telephone or pick up additional score report forms in the College Advising Office or go online. Releasing Score Choice and reporting scores to the colleges are two different procedures. You are responsible for both. In order to fill out these score report forms, you must know your CEEB registration number (found on the blue student copy, which contains your scores and which you received in the mail) and the code numbers of the colleges to which you are applying (found in the SAT registration bulletin).

Let's hear the perception of an Ivy dean of admissions on Score Choice before you make your decision on what to do about those senior year SAT IIs. In his "Most Frequently Asked Questions" piece, Princeton's Dean Hargadon cautions students not to use Score Choice senior year. He writes, "This past year, by the time those applicants who had opted for Score Choice received their scores and only then asked the testing agency to release them to the colleges, many of the scores simply arrived too late, i.e., after the applications of many of those students had already been reviewed." Now listen. You don't want that to happen to you. Take the dean's advice and realize that the colleges use the three highest SAT II scores anyway, and therefore you aren't taking any risk, as they know your earlier scores. Not to mention that many students forget that they had opted for Score Choice when they registered, and never do send them in.

Secondary School Report Form

Most applications will have a Secondary School Report (SSR) form. Fill out the top part of this form with your name and address and take it to your college or guidance office. Your Secondary School Report form will be mailed to the college by your high school in time to meet your deadline and will include the following:

1. Transcript (including courses and grades).

2. Test data (unofficial SAT I and released SAT II scores). Some high schools no longer send a copy of your SAT scores; they rely on you to send your official scores from the College Board.

3. Your high school letter of recommendation signed by your principal or guidance counselor (college advisor), or both.

4. Your high school profile (a description of your school, information on test scores of your class, GPAs, grade distribution of your class, and a list of colleges where previous classes have matriculated).

5. Some high schools send teacher recommendations along with the other reports. Don't drive the college office crazy asking if your SSR went out or not. On the other hand, it's reasonable for you to ask when you return from your winter holiday if your stuff went out. You'll be happy to know that the dean of admissions does not hold you responsible for late transcripts and records that are sent from your school.

Teacher Recommendations

Most colleges require a teacher recommendation, and some require two. It is most important that you choose teachers who know you best to write your recommendations. Sometimes a college will specify that the recommendations come from particular teachers. Try to get the two teachers in different areas of learning. Here's what you do:

1. Ask the teacher if she or he will write a recommendation for you.

2. Give the teacher the proper form filled in as requested, with an addressed, stamped envelope for each college, with plenty of time to write it. On the envelope, pencil in the deadline date for the particular college. A teacher may write one letter,

photocopy it, and attach it to each of the forms for different colleges. *The same teachers will write all of your recommendations.* Don't hesitate to ask them, as they will expect you to use them for all of your applications. Keep in mind that teachers have many recommendations to write. If you don't ask them early (with three weeks to write it), many will have to say "no," simply because they are overcommitted with other college recommendations.

3. After you get your college decisions, tell the teachers of your acceptances and thank them for writing the recommendations. Don't forget to keep your teachers informed! They are pleased to write the letters for you, but want to be kept up to date with the results.

Other Letters of Recommendation

It's tempting to send letters of recommendation from all of those people in high places who love you—your clergy, the cardinal of Chicago, summer and after-school boss, U.S. senator, neighbors, your parent's senior law partner, the head doctor in the university lab who supervised your summer science project—but do not send more letters than asked for *unless* the letter writers have a strong connection with that particular college. In most cases, reading those "love letters" just takes valuable time—time that could be better spent reading what *you* write and what your classroom teachers and school are writing about you. On the other hand, having people in high places with a strong connection to the particular college write letters of recommendation can be a strategy that will make a big difference for *qualified* students. A college trustee is a strong connection. A friend of the university president is a strong connection. An alumnus or alumna who gives a lot of money to the college (development) is a strong connection. A grandparent is considered a legacy, and that is also a strong connection. If you have a sister currently at Northwestern, send her into the admissions office in mid-February to talk to Shep Shanley about you and the match for his campus. If your father graduated from Brown, or your mother from Holy Cross, their letters can make a difference. These letters should be short—one page. Letters are better than phone calls because they will be added to your folder for more than one person on the committee to read. A phone call is easily lost in the thousands of pieces of paper flying around the admissions dean's office in February. And your legacy parents should write about you and what they know of the campus culture—in other words, the match. That's the piece that they know best and what the college can't get from anybody else. All of the strong connection letters should be sent around Valentine's Day (a little "winning the heart" symbolism can't hurt), close enough to decision time so the admissions committee won't forget and not too close to decision time when the deans are so crazed with overwork that they won't remember to file the letter.

Application Deadlines: Early, Rolling, and Regular

It used to be that most students applied to college at the same time— regular decision time. Times have changed. Now the majority of students get in early or late decision, that is, early or they come in late off the wait list after May 1. Many public universities get students in any time of year on the rolling admissions plan. Let's take a closer look at what's best for you—not necessarily what everyone else is doing—but the best strategy for you to get the options you want.

Early Action (EA)

First, there's early action (EA), a program whereby you will apply by the first or middle of November and will receive an early decision in mid-December but are not obligated to enroll if admitted (you may also be denied or deferred early). Harvard and Chicago are best known for EA; other well-known schools with EA programs include Boston College, Georgetown, MIT, and Notre Dame. The risk with Early Action programs is you can be denied on the basis of your junior year and not deferred into their regular pool of applicants to be evaluated by your senior year record.

Early Decision (ED)

The early plan that you hear most about is early decision (ED). In this program you apply by the first or middle of November and receive an early decision in mid-December. You are obligated to enroll if admitted (if the financial aid is sufficient) and to withdraw all other college applications. You may also be denied or deferred. Increasingly, colleges are offering a second or "late" early decision, with decisions given in February, and some even a "late-late" early decision.

Let's look at early decision as it is: Early plans at selective colleges are for outstanding students. For early decision, highly selective colleges take from 35 percent to 65 percent of their freshman class, meaning the top dogs, crème de la crème, those with top grades in a rigorous program, and big-time testers. If you are not at the top but want the college to know it is your first choice, there are many ways to tell them: Write it on your application or in your essay, and tell the admissions officer during your interview. It's not to your advantage to apply early, if say, you don't have the numbers, if you don't have a chance in the tough early competition. You are not allowed second thoughts about other colleges. Some applicants are rejected altogether, that is, they are denied rather than deferred by mid-December, losing the opportunity to submit better text scores and higher grades earned during the senior year. It's also devastating to be rejected in December. Talk over the early decision possibility *carefully* at home and with your school counselor to verify that you have the "numbers" needed from your high school to get in early. It's getting to be such a big thing that I'd like you to consider the downside of early decision, which is discussed in chapter 7.

Rolling Admissions

Rolling admissions is an admissions policy by which the dean evaluates and decides upon applicants as soon as their application files are complete. This continues until the class is full. Colleges with rolling admissions usually promise a decision within six weeks. Public universities are often rolling, although they often hold the decision until spring for out-of-state students, and the dates tend to vary each year. Some colleges consider a complete file at the end of junior year and others wait for first-term senior grades. Because many of the state universities are on rolling admissions, and students tend to apply early, some colleges may fill their housing and main campus by January. The sooner the better for rolling admissions. If you have already decided that they are on your final list, your application for universities such as Michigan, Penn State, and Wisconsin should be completed by November 1. Treat rolling admissions as early decision deadlines.

Mailing Applications

It is *your* responsibility to mail your own applications as soon as they are completed. Your high school will send your transcript, but you are responsible for telling your guidance counselor the deadlines by which each college must receive your grades and reports. Regardless of when your high school gets their records out, your applications should be sent as soon as you have completed them. Be sure to get your application in before the deadline, and remember to photocopy them before you send them. *Exceptions:* There are a handful of colleges who want your school to mail your application. The college will send you a large envelope and ask that your application and the school records be mailed at the same time. In that case, your guidance office will mail your part of the application and your application check together with the school reports.

Resist January Add-Ons

It's January of senior year. Your applications are in the mail. You have personalized the college process as best you can. You are well on your way to winning many college deans' hearts. There's nothing more to do. At the last minute you dreaded to let go and drop that envelope into the mailbox. Now the long wait for early April has begun. The dreams have begun too. Seniors are famous for their college decision dreams; they begin from the moment that they mail their applications. January is when seniors all over the country rush into their college counselor and say, "I'd better add just one more college." Your parents call your guidance counselor to say, "I was at a New Year's party and talked to my niece who goes to Cornell, or I was talking to my sister at my nephew's bar mitzvah in Dallas—she has a neighbor who goes to Reed," or "My sister from Philadelphia, whose children go to Haverford, called and they thought that Susie should have applied there too. It's not too late, what harm can one more application do?"

Resist the temptation to send just one more application. The urge to apply to another college is the first sign of anxiety in the waiting process. It's true. Taking action helps reduce anxiety. But adding a college each month is not the most constructive action you can take. You have a college list, and it's a well-balanced college list. You have researched your possibilities, talked endlessly with your parents, your friends, teachers, and college counselor. Your college list represents a consistency in type of college environment—those colleges where you will be most productive. It also represents a range in the competition for admissions. In other words, it's a balanced list. Adding another college from out of nowhere, often from someone who doesn't have a clue about the logic of your choices, does not work toward the good of getting your best options.

> **Resist the temptation to send just one more application.**

There is, however, an important action you can take to quench that anxious feeling that you need to be doing something. That action is to concentrate on the colleges to which you have already applied. That action is designed to increase your odds for getting into the colleges on your list. You can begin right now by working harder on each subject you are taking.

College admissions deans will welcome significant new information about applicants before they make their decisions in mid-March. You can send an exceptional paper or report a significant achievement to the college dean before mid-March. You can write an unusual paper, compose a poem, a song, a short story; research an event in history; create a piece of art or painting; construct an outstanding experiment in science; win races on the swim team, establish a new basketball record; write a play in French, or tell about your independent study project. In other words, you can further distinguish yourself from the pack in some academic, athletic, leadership, or artistic way. Begin now—as soon as you have the urge to add another college to your college list. Talk with your teachers and ask them to help you to present a significant piece of new work to the college. Please note: The key word here is "significant." Significant doesn't mean more of the same. It doesn't mean to add quantity to what you have already sent the college rep or dean.

Let me tell you a sad story. Ben Z. applied to Columbia. He was right up there with his numbers: high 700s across the board, A and B+ record in a rigorous curriculum from a top competitive private school. He had sent a wonderful portfolio of his writing to the Columbia rep. The Columbia rep and I talked on the phone; Ben was looking good in the pool. Colleges love writers—male writers even have an edge, as female mathematicians do. Ben couldn't control his waiting anxiety, so he brought me a stack of literary magazines and newspapers in which he had been published to send to the rep so the rep could really see how good he was. No amount of "The rep will hate that, Ben, admissions officers don't want a stack of magazines and newspapers, and besides that, you have already sent a terrific portfolio with most of those stories," could dissuade Ben from sending his magazines. A few days later the phone rings. "Joyce, I just received fifty pounds of scrap paper from your Ben. That's going to hurt him. Haven't you taught your students not to send me this kind of baled garbage that I have to get rid of?" Needless to say, Ben was denied at Columbia.

Don't waste your resources (time and energy) on symptoms of anxiety by running scared and adding a college helter-skelter to your list. Instead, build on the firm foundation you've been working on since first grade to establish your academic credibility. You have done a solid piece of work constructing your college list through self-assessment and college research. Be confident! Have courage! Send the college dean a significant piece of new work and then go out and run around your school track until you are ready to think about something else.

CHAPTER 10

The Interview

tudents tend to dread the college interview more than they do the dentist. When they come back to report about the interview, they are often disappointed because it turned out to be an information session selling the college rather than an interview for getting to know the student. Or other times a student will fly a long distance to visit a college and only to get an interview with a student. Now that's the high school side of the issue. Rice's Richard Stabell pointed out to me that their seniors are well-trained student interviewers and are very helpful to the process. And Duke's Christoph Guttentag agreed that if students are interviewing applicants, it's very important for the high school student to know if it's an evaluative or an information-giving interview. Is it required or recommended?

The truth is that your parents tend to overrate the value of the interview, and the colleges tend to underrate them. You will notice that your parents will ask you a million interview questions, "Are you ready for the interview? Shouldn't you have a practice interview at a college where you won't apply? Does your guidance counselor give you practice

> **Your parents tend to overrate the value of the interview, and the colleges tend to underrate them.**

interviews at school? Here—read this book on interviews!" Parents just can't believe that their charming, fascinating, brilliant child will not wow the admissions dean and be accepted on the spot—if only she could have an interview with the dean of admissions. College deans, on the other hand, tend to say that the interview affirms the rest of the applicant's file, and unless they spot a freak, it doesn't usually make a difference in acceptance. But hey! Don't we all know by now that the unconscious is always at work, and if the dean hits it off with you, won't he read your whole folder with a smile on his face? Of course he will. Here is just one more opportunity to win the heart of the college admissions dean by personalizing your application. This is a chance to show the inner you behind your numbers. But puh-leeze, try not to read too much into the interview, such as "We were supposed to meet for thirty minutes and I was in there for over an hour!" A lot of disappointment comes out of hitting it off with the marketing man, who of course is friendly and interested, and putting forth his best efforts to get you to apply to his school—regardless of your academic record!

The Unconscious Power of the Interview

Let's face it, colleges are clear about what they are looking for in your application, essay, SAT scores, teacher recommendations, and the secondary school report. They are not so clear about what they want from your interview, if they want an interview, and who does the interview. And they are not at all clear about how they use the interview. It's easy to agree that the use and value of an interview varies more than any other aspect of the college admissions process. Typical of the remarks made by the deans of admissions who give interviews is this one from Wylie Mitchell, Dean of Admissions at Bates College: "Evaluative interview notes are the last thing in the applicant's folder, and the admissions committee reads them last. If there is a discrepancy between the interview and the high school's recommendation, we call the guidance counselor, and if we can't reach anyone at the high school, we go with the school's report, knowing that we had a very short time with the student."

But, wait. Let's always remember this: What colleges *say* they want and what they want are sometimes two different things. What they wanted last year and what they want this year and will want next year are often three different things. Let's listen to Ivy League Director of Admissions Eric J. Kaplan at the University of Pennsylvania: "I wish I could give unqualified answers, but I can't. And herein lies the frustration for all of the weary students and their parents. The objectives of an institution are like a moving target. They can change almost annually to reflect its priorities. One cannot adequately prepare to be a top candidate for an Ivy League college by cultivating a set of skills that meet today's priorities; tomorrow's may be very different." Not to be blamed for not knowing what they really want, admissions deans, like most people, don't know how they make decisions. Add their different institutional priorities each year and they become moving targets. They often would not admit that their unconscious is fast at work, as their gut tells them what to do while their head spins quickly to catch up with a rationalization of "why" they decided as they did. This is true for how people buy a car, how they rent an apartment, choose a friend, and how admissions deans decide which 20 percent of the 80 percent qualifieds will get into their freshman class.

Because of this human behavior trait, I make a point of teaching my high school seniors the unconscious part of the decision-making process once the numbers (curriculum, grades, and testing) are in place. I don't have to remind you that the selective colleges choose one-fourth and less of the qualified students who apply to their colleges. Even though the numbers of the freshman class will remain relatively the same, the numbers of college admissions officers reading applications aren't increasing to keep up with the rapidly increasing numbers of applicants. If you could sit around any selective college admissions' committee table, you would quickly learn that the hand of the admissions officer shoots up for a "YES!" if and when the student has personalized her application. The applicant that the dean recognizes is one of the 25 percent who will get admitted from the qualified pool. Unlike what the SAT prep businesses want the public to think, it never comes down to who has a 700 verbal over a 650; once they get in the verbal 650 range, the numbers game is all over, and it's the student who wins the heart of the admissions dean that gets in.

The student who wins the dean's heart does it mostly through the essay, the written word. After all, the written word documents how a student thinks. You also can win the dean's heart through your application, although many students fall short—those short answers are too often written with great haste. As I've mentioned before and probably before that, in all too many instances, the student loses out on the application opportunity to win a heart.

The Spoken Word

Coming right in there after the numbers and written word is the spoken word component. The spoken word comes in several forms: The interview is the most formal of the spoken word, but verbal interaction anywhere and anytime can build toward winning (or losing) the heart of the admissions dean.

Interviews and getting together in person with a college admissions dean or rep at college fairs, college receptions, or college information sessions, when the college admissions dean visits your high school, and when you visit the college campus are all part of the blah-blah factor (spoken word component). In other words, to win the dean's heart you have to be aware of the verbal factor. Your verbal encounters go beyond the formal interview, to include *anytime* you have a personal interaction with the college admissions dean, whether it is on campus, at your high school, at the Yale Club in New York, at the Harvard Club in Chicago, or on neutral territory.

An Interview Survey

Because nothing varies more from campus to campus than the interview policy, I ran my own survey. Consider, for example, that Bates evaluates and gives a numerical rating to their interviews that counts as much as a classroom teacher's recommendation; the University of Pennsylvania grants interviews only to legacies; and Tufts has completely dropped all on-campus interviews as they can't keep up with the numbers of applicants or with training the staff for the interviewing skills necessary to evaluate them. I asked most of the 101 colleges to which my Class of 2001 students applied if their interview is:

> ▶ An information session—selling the college?
>
> ▶ Evaluative? And if so, is the interview: Described in essay format? Evaluated on a numerical scale? Evaluated by an admissions officer, a student, or the alumni?
>
> ▶ Required, recommended, or non-existent?
>
> ▶ Initiated by the student or college?

The answers were mixed. And that makes interviews confusing for students. Confusing means that they vary a lot from college to college. Confusion also produces anxiety. Let's see what you need to know about college interviews to cut through some of this confusion. Some colleges say interviews count a lot. Some say they are information sessions and not real interviews. Some say they are just to keep the alumni happy. Some interviews are even done by students on work-study jobs in the admissions office. Well, do they really count? It depends. It depends on the policy of the college: Is it an information session or is it an evaluative interview? The point for you to keep in mind is that, no matter what they say, the blah–blah factor *always counts* on some level.

Here are some examples of how the interview policy varies from college to college:

> ▶ Amherst interviews about 30 percent of their early admissions, 15 percent of their regular admissions, and most of their transfers.
>
> ▶ Barnard interviews and evaluates the interview in written form. Bates does too.

▶ Brandeis recommends an on-campus interview until February 1, they evaluate numerically from 1–5 and put the written evaluation into the student's file, and a student can request an alumni interview starting in mid-May for juniors.

▶ Bryn Mawr strongly recommends an on-campus interview by their staff; about 75 percent of their applicants are interviewed, and students can get off-campus alumnae interviews.

▶ Bucknell recommends an on-campus interview. Director Mark Davies says that interviews can help in admissions, not to mention it shows that the student has interest by going to the campus and thinking ahead to arrange for the interview. They have an interview training manual for their alumni, who interview about 50 percent of the applicants off campus.

▶ Connecticut College strongly encourages on-campus interviews. They are looking for passion and explanation of the grades. The admissions staff goes to New York City in January to interview applicants. The interviews are evaluated and written up, the yield (number of accepted students who enroll) is 50 percent to 60 percent of those who interview on campus. Twelve college seniors are selected to be formally trained to interview on campus.

▶ Dartmouth's admissions staff interviews and evaluates almost 75 percent of the applicants both on and off campus in the fall. They look for consistency in the students' files with how they present themselves verbally as well as their written presentation.

▶ Emory does not do interviews on campus or off.

▶ Georgetown requires an alumni interview. The admissions dean travels to alumni all over the country to train the alumni for interviewing about the life experience of the seventeen-year-old. They find that about 10 percent of the applicants are different from their written record. That is, the dean's perception of the student doesn't often change because of the interview. There is a very strong alumni association, which has developed a training booklet for interviewing Georgetown applicants.

▶ Grinnell highly recommends an interview on or off campus with alumni. They evaluate about 50 percent of the applicants. The teacher's letter counts more, but the interview evaluation comes in right after the letters.

▶ Kenyon strongly recommends an interview. Dean of Admissions John Anderson says that the interview demonstrates a strong interest in Kenyon. Ninety percent of the interviews confirm the written record. Students are interviewed by staff, college seniors, and alumni, all of whom are trained and evaluate the interview. Two-thirds of the applicants are interviewed.

▶ Middlebury's interviews are nonevaluative, but they are written and placed in the applicant's file. The staff interviews about 2,600 students, and the alumni interview about 3,000. Director of Admissions John Hanson expects a campus visit from students who live within reasonable travel distance and he has designated funds to assist students who can't afford the travel fare.

▶ Mount Holyoke highly recommends an interview. Dean Diane Anci says that they take the interview very seriously, and they train alumnae to interview off campus. The dean says that often an applicant is very compelling at the inteview, or they find they have real reservations about the candidate. She takes pride in their interviewing process and remarks, "Mount Holyoke does good interviews on campus that matter."

▶ Princeton alumni interview about 60 percent of the applicants. On-campus interviews are conducted in small groups.

- ▶ Skidmore interviews until February 1 of senior year, interviews are highly recommended, they are evaluative and seen as the third dimension of an applicant; 40 percent of the applicants are interviewed.

- ▶ Smith College highly recommends them but interviews are optional.

- ▶ Stanford doesn't do alumni or staff interviews, although they encourage campus visits.

- ▶ Swarthmore strongly recommends on-campus interviews by mid-December of senior year. The alumni evaluate with numbers and description, but there is not a formal weighting of the interview in the selection process.

- ▶ Tufts strongly recommends off-campus alumni interviews. They are especially interested in hearing about academic interests and extracurricular achievements. About 70 percent of their applicants have an alumni interview.

- ▶ Union College strongly recommends on-campus interviews beginning in February of junior year. Admissions officer Ann Flemming Brown says she likes to hear in-depth discussions about the curriculum and the passions of the student. They hold regional receptions with interviews in Portland, Maine; New York City; Chicago; Los Angeles; and San Francisco. Alumni give interviews and write a description as well as quantify the interview. "Here's an important statistic," says Brown, "Ninety percent of those enrolled had an interview." Hey, seniors, how's that statistic for personalizing the college selection process?

- ▶ Vanderbilt does not interview.

- ▶ Vassar does not require them, but students can usually get an interview.

Do Interviews Count?

Well, what did you learn from this great variety of interview policies? What are you going to do if the colleges where you are going to apply aren't in this survey group? Here's what you can use from this survey: The policies vary so much that you will have to ask the college admissions dean (a) do you require an interview? (b) where can I get an interview? (c) is the interview evaluated? and (d) do most applicants get an interview? Finally, if you live within three hours' drive of the college, get an interview on campus so that you can be counted as one applicant who is interested enough to come to campus and ask for an interview.

Need it be said that you won't be able to find a "right way" to interview or a book to tell you how to interview? No matter which part of the process you are working on, you must always keep in mind that, given the great diversity of American colleges, colleges do not all want the same kind of student. Likewise, a particular college doesn't want their students all alike, and each year they may have different priorities for the students that they do want. As in the application and essay, your focus should be on finding and trusting your own voice, that is, the voice of a teenager telling the dean about his or her special talents. Your written word (essay, application, classroom papers) and your spoken word (interview, college dean encounters) are found within you, not by reading other students' essays or an interview format. What's in *you* is what the deans want.

Juniors and seniors: Don't dread the interview. Think conversation—this is not a grilling session or a search for right answers. Whatever you say in the interview must make sense to you! If you aren't comfortable asking how this college differs from other ones that sound similar to you, don't ask it. If you would rather talk about current events that you

> Don't dread the interview. Think conversation—this is not a grilling session or a search for right answers.

know well from reading a daily newspaper than discuss a book, turn the question around and talk about what you know best.

You will probably see more variation in the interview policy than in any other area of the application process. Just as you are responsible for knowing the particular tests required for each college, you are also responsible for knowing the interview policy. When you're on campus, take a campus tour, attend an information session, see the dorms, find out where the students hang out and talk to them. Try to schedule an interview. Try to schedule your interview from June through December of your senior year. Call the admissions dean in March or April of junior year for a summer appointment. You can get the names and phone numbers of the admissions rep who is responsible for your high school from your guidance or college office. Summer of your junior year is the best time to schedule interviews; in the fall you are too involved with your challenging academics, writing college applications and term papers, and participating in fall sports. You need to make appointments as early as two to three months ahead of time, and remember that a weekend interview in the fall of your senior year at the selective colleges is almost impossible to come by. Colleges that require an interview will initiate the process *after* you have applied. Besides the on-campus interviews, others that you may well encounter are the student interview, the alumni interview, the group interview, the special-interest interview, and the audition. (The special-interest and audition interviews are usually for the performing arts and sports.) When you find out the policy of the particular college on your final list, you will learn which kind of an interview you will have. If you have a choice between an on-campus interview with the admissions staff or an off-campus alumni interview, always go with the on-campus admissions staff. Even though they both put an evaluative report into your folder, only the admissions staff sits around that committee table and raises their hand to say "yes" to your application. In all of these interviews, your goal is always the same: (a) to distinguish yourself and (b) to show high interest in their college.

Have some hard facts at hand about the academics and any of your special interests in music, theater, sports, or publications, and have some hard questions to ask that aren't easily answered in the view books. Showing strong interest is more and more an important factor in being accepted by selective colleges.

Interview Tips

Read the college guides and catalog ahead of time so that you will know important things about the college *before* you get to the interview. Have some questions in mind that are specific for that college. Be prepared to talk about your strengths and traits that need improvement, as well as your interests and special talents. Remember that interviews are a two-way exchange. Try to think of the interview as a conversation rather than a question-and-answer session. Here are some tips:

▶ Don't chew gum. Practice by not chewing gum when you go to college rep visits at your high school.

▶ Watch your language. Avoid "like," "cool," "whatever.'" At least cut down on the numbers of times you use these words.

▶ If you have a straight A record in AP courses, have taken twenty-three solids, have at least 750–750 SAT scores, and have a book coming out on globalization, it doesn't matter too much what you wear. But if you're like most students with a little less than the above, a good impression always helps. Clean school clothes, not torn or ripped, are fine. Look together. Arrive on time, shake hands firmly, sit and stand straight, and act confident and happy to be there. Cool doesn't sell. Sullen doesn't either; the dean will know that your mother made you be there.

▶ Admissions interviews are your opportunity to sell yourself. Make a friend of the interviewer. Look her in the eye. Be straightforward and relaxed in your conversation. Don't try to get at "what they want to hear." Be confident that there are no "right" answers or directions for the interview to go. They want to know you better. Your attitude toward learning is what they want to know most. Do you have a sense of humor? Do you have the ability to overcome tough situations? Are you resilient after getting a bad grade, or do you get mad at the teacher and stop working? What do you know about this college? Are you the kind of student who can take advantage of the educational opportunities at this college? How high is your interest in attending this college? What kind of match will you make in this college community? How will you manage your time and life when you get away from home and on your own? How will you spend your out-of-class time? What are your values? What are you bringing to the college community? The more you like you, the more the interviewer (and others) will too!

▶ Have clear goals that you are able to discuss honestly. Some common questions they may ask: What interests you about this college? What are you looking for in a college? What are your educational goals? Why should we accept you? What do you expect to contribute to our college community?

▶ Don't give excuses for your grades or tell how you're going to do better next semester (wishful thinking). Lead from your strengths. For example, talk about your love for reading, for sports, for a beautiful campus, for Latin, for the Net, for politics, your pride in your family, your achievements, your dog-training techniques, your summer school experience, your snowboarding awards, your favorite newspaper, your favorite section of the newspaper, the business you started.

▶ Take time to listen to the questions and answer them directly. It's hard, but try not to worry about silence. Collect your thoughts. Tell the admissions person that you are eager to go to college and what you like about *this* college.

Go to the interview with your goal clearly in your mind: to distinguish yourself and to be sure that the dean of admissions is clear that you are interested in getting into his college. Trust yourself. You are the one that the college wants to get to know, and if you are comfortable with the conversations that you have with the dean of admissions, you can be sure that you did well. Get right in there with the blah-blah factor every chance you have in order to distinguish that fascinating *you* behind your great numbers!

CHAPTER 11

Late Decision
(Wait Listed!)

High school seniors read and hear an awful lot of talk about early action, early decision, early notification, early this and early that. I call it "first down." Sports talk. On the other hand, you never read or hear about late decision—or getting into college off the wait list after May 1. I call it "stealing home." More sports talk. Getting in off the wait list is the spring sport of the college application season. Colleges don't like to talk about it. They don't include "late decision" in their information sessions to students and parents, but you should know about late decision because a significant percentage of the freshman class comes in from the wait list. You should also know about late decisions before spring arrives with April letters informing you that you are on wait-list status. You have to be ready for late decision in order to take advantage of the process. Your mind must be open. Your psyche set. There's no giving up until the wait list—the late decision—is closed.

A smaller and smaller proportion of incoming classes are getting into college on regular admission in April. As many selective colleges take up to and over 60 percent early, and other colleges take up to 33 percent of their class from their wait list, we are talking about a significant percentage of the class getting in on an early or late decision!

When I tell a senior that he has a 50 percent chance to get into Johns Hopkins, for example, I mean before September, not necessarily as an early (December) or regular (April) acceptance. It is not to your advantage to "have to know" your college decision early in December or regular in April. You must be psyched ahead of time for the long haul, for the whole nine yards, and even for overtime if necessary. The college selection process is a process that, like any real challenge, builds character. And character never builds quickly.

The college selection process is a process that builds character. And character never builds quickly.

Some years a lot more late decision (wait list) activity happens than other years. Whenever there is a new director of admissions or an interim director at a college, you can count on it. If a college isn't sure of their "yield" (number of enrolled students from the accepted list), or if their yield is down and many chosen students do not accept their kind invitation, the colleges use the wait list and late decision as a safety net. Some years a college can take as many as three hundred students off the wait list to get the freshman numbers that they need. Because of a late decision, many a student goes to a college that's different from the one they had fantasized about all senior year. And yet when those wait-listed seniors learn more about that college option, they find that the wait list worked better for them than their original preference. If you still aren't sure if

you want the wait-listed college or not, you can decide what you want to do after you get off the wait list. You will have a choice between the wait-listed and your "deposited" college, that is, the college where you've already been accepted and paid your deposit to hold your spot in the incoming class. Many students ask—so let me say right here—if you get off the wait list, you don't necessarily have to go there!

Let's say that you decide to stay on two wait lists. If you stay on a wait list, you will want to do your best to be accepted. Doing your best means more than returning the requested card to accept wait-list status. Best effort means writing a letter along with the card that you return. In that short letter, tell the admissions dean that it's disappointing not to have been accepted. Give an academic reason why you are still interested in, for example, Sarah Lawrence (something other than you love Westchester County or your best friend goes there). Add something new that the college doesn't know: provide latest grades (if they went up), enclose a graded English paper—even if not an A it will document the kind of work you do and the kind of instruction you receive. Enclose a poem, short story, or school newspaper article that you wrote since you applied. And finally, end your letter with a statement that you plan to be there in September. Write that letter assuming you are going to get off the wait list and onto the accept list. In recent years, some wait lists were still moving in August, even though most colleges agree to close their wait list by June 30. If your wait-list college is the college you still want after all of your decisions are in, hang in there and keep sending something new to express your continued interest. Call or send something at least every two weeks, and keep your energy high when talking to the admissions dean. Give the wait-list action your best shot. If you cared enough to apply in the first place, don't let up now and do half a job. Put your two best feet forward. Be creative about it. Getting off the wait list is like stealing home—it's a great challenge and fun!

Sports talk isn't important. But an athlete's behavior and attitude *are* an important model: Get in there and give your best. Be in good enough shape to stay until overtime has been played out. Be in psychological shape to go the extra inning after a tie—until a late decision has been made. Early decision (first down) to regular decision to late decision (stealing home)

> Getting off the wait list is like stealing home—it's a great challenge and fun!

are three different ball games. Like athletes, you can go into the competition knowing the different strategies of the three separate ball games for the best advantage. Let's remember that America's top three hundred colleges have so many outstanding students applying that many of the admit and wait-list students are interchangeable. Colleges are looking for reasons to take one wait-listed student over another. It's up to you to give it to them!

CHAPTER 12

Transfers

There are a lot of good reasons why students transfer. Many students will tell you that they transferred because of their major or because they couldn't afford the college. But most often, although she'd never admit it, the student didn't do her research and it just plain wasn't a good match—she didn't fit in. The students weren't her kind of people. Still others transfer to "trade up," to go to a stronger academic college. Don't worry about why you want to transfer. Transferring is big time in American colleges and universities. Let's look at a few students who transferred.

I had a student who was dying to go to Colgate from New York City. She got there and found it "too rural," "too remote," "too fraternity," so she transferred to Barnard (as a high school senior she swore she would *never* go to a woman's college). After a year at Barnard she missed all her Colgate pals, the rural, the remote, the fraternities, so back she went to Colgate to earn her degree. Might I add that she is now a graduate student in religion at Columbia University (back to Barnard). I had another student who was dying to go to Wesleyan, but he didn't get in. He went to a less competitive college where he took no math, no science, and no foreign language his first year. He got a B average and waltzed into Wesleyan his sophomore year. It's much easier to get into the selective colleges as a sophomore than as a fresh-man! I spoke to a transfer student at a top public university who said he came for an architecture program, but they cut the program after his first semester there. I asked why he didn't transfer, and his response was, "Because I love it here." A student transferred from Pitzer to Reed, where she became an art history major. At that time, however, there was no studio art major, which is what she decided she wanted. She stayed anyway because, as she put it, "It's where I want to be." (Studio art is currently the third largest major at Reed.) Lastly, some students transfer because they change. One young man couldn't wait to go to Michigan for the Big Ten football games, the great variety of strong undergraduate courses, a big enough place where everyone wouldn't know his name and keep after him every second. After two years of enjoying all of those things, he decided that he wanted a small, focused community where he could get in-depth conversation all the time about environmental issues, and so he transferred to Bowdoin.

What's my point? When the match (campus culture to personality) is right, the program just doesn't make that much difference in a liberal arts college. Liberal arts closes no doors. Liberal arts leads to everything. A major in English literature, mathematics, chemistry, biology, psychology, foreign language, economics, or religion leads to every career in the world.

> A major in English literature, mathematics, chemistry, biology, psychology, foreign language, economics, or religion leads to every career in the world.

It doesn't matter why you want to transfer; what matters is that you have the freedom and the option to transfer and know how to go about it. Usually you can transfer up to two years of undergraduate work. Things are differ-ent in the application process from high school because you now have a college record. Usually the application is due in March or April for a fall transfer. Some colleges take a January transfer. Check it out with the admissions dean.

The new college will be more interested in your college grades than they will in your high school record or SATs. Even though the dean of admissions will be interested in what you did outside of the classroom, it's your personal statement that is read the most carefully after your college transcript. It has to be good. It has to be convincing. What did you learn about yourself and the world in those one or two years at college? Why do you want to transfer? Why do you especially want to transfer to the college to which you are applying? Be sure you have strong academic reasons for the transfer—get the catalog, meet a professor or two, and know what you are looking for. Look at the *Insider's Guide* and see how many transfers are admitted. The college admissions dean and a staff member in charge of transfers expect more insights out of you than they would from a high school student. And of course you have more insight, so that won't be an obstacle. Recommendations should come from professors at your first college, not from your high school teachers. If you have a friend who is a student in the school where you want to go, send him in to meet the transfer admissions officer and put in a good word for you.

Before you go, find out how many transfers will be coming in your class and where you can live. (If you don't yet have friends there, try to live on campus at least the first semester so you can easily and naturally meet a lot of students.) Try to go on campus before you apply, go around to the department where you plan to major, and meet some of the other majors and professors.

In the meantime, carefully check chapter 3—What's Out There? so that you consider all of your options before you make your next move. Remember: It's your college academic record and your personal statement that will get you in where you want to go. Don't hesitate to get over there, meet the transfer admissions officer, and win her heart!

PART III

A Word to the Wise Parents

CHAPTER 13

A Parenting Challenge

Iknow. Parents have very different concerns than their sons and daughters about going off to college. Seldom does anyone talk about the trauma of having a child leave home. So intent is the "Where am I going to college?" that the dread of losing your child lurks silently in your heart. And, of course, there are money questions too. Is it going to be worth the price? Am I willing to pay $150,000 for a college that isn't even Ivy League? Will my child be safe in those coed dorms, in cars with kids drinking and driving? Will my child be safe in some other part of the country where we don't have any friends or relatives? And does he know what he wants? When does preparing for a career come into the conversation? Where can we begin to address all of your questions? Let's start from the beginning. Your son or daughter is leaving home. Going off to college. You want them to have the very best.

Hired Gun: The Private Consultant

Many parents ask, "Should I hire a private consultant to help with this crucial decision for my child? After all, I want what's best for him." My question to you is, "Does your son have a college advisor or guidance counselor who handles the college process at school?" If he is in a private school, you can be sure that the school thinks they have the best in college advising. After all, like it or not, their reputation is often built on their college list. If your child is in a public school that has a guidance counselor that deals with all the problems of high school including curriculum choices, behavior problems, poor grades, relationship problems between teachers and students, teachers and parents, students and parents, students are often short-changed in college advising. If a college counselor has a load of three hundred seniors or more and doesn't have time for individual attention, then outside help may make sense. In fact, public school guidance counselors often recommend the best consultants in their region. It is not a dilemma for outsiders to work with overextended guidance counselors in areas where their expertise is needed—and often purchased under contract from the school. The private consultants' efforts can fill a great need when they are able to help students and families who don't have a clue

> The college selection process is more than your child choosing where she is going next year—it also provides seniors with an educational opportunity that includes a lot of important developmental tasks that they most need in order to grow up enough to leave home.

about the college selection process and can't get what they need to know from their schools. If your children go to a high school where nobody has gone out of state to college for the past two years, then you may want to get outside help. You surely will also want to take a closer look at chapter 3—What's Out There?

Like all things in our imperfect world, even though we want America's high school teenagers to have the privilege of a good education, strong teachers, and a terrific college counselor who knows what she is doing and has time to work with each senior, we don't always get what we need and want. Moreover, the gap between public and private schools is probably at its widest in their college selection programs.

The college selection process is more than your child choosing where she is going next year—it also provides seniors with an educational opportunity that includes a lot of important developmental tasks that they most need in order to grow up enough to leave home. Making decisions about college presents young people with a situation in which they must learn how to distinguish themselves from their peers and how to highlight those distinguishing characteristics in writing. This process builds character and teaches seniors a skill they will use throughout their lives. As an educator, I see the college selection process as an independent study in decision making, a learning experience that prepares students to choose the environments in which they will be most productive and happy. They can choose from hundreds of different campus cultures, none of which is right for everyone, and all of which are wonderful for someone. It is an independent study in which seniors much choose from their options (the colleges from which they were accepted) and consider those options even when they differ from their family's choices.

> The college selection process is an independent study in decision making.

What happens to this developmental task when an outsider is brought into the loop of student, high school, and colleges? How does an independent counselor affect the senior in high school? If a family is willing to spend the money, many will ask, "What harm will it do?" "What harm will it do" is a question that often arises during the college selection process. What harm will it to do apply early? What harm will it do to apply to a dream school? What harm will it do to apply to eighteen colleges? The questions are always asked by parents as if they didn't have a downside.

Here is the harm to the student: I have never had a senior come in and announce with pride or empowerment that he now has an educational consultant! Never. In surveying my colleagues on this question, I find students are confused (should I be relieved to have another point of view or worried that my counselor won't like it?), embarrassed (it's their parents' idea), and feel deceitful (they avoid their college advisor). I first learned that one of my students had a private consultant by reading an article in *New York Magazine*. The point of the article was that the outside consultant knows a lot more tricks or can play the angles, such as "apply to Cornell's agriculture college rather than to arts and science," as if the admissions professionals at Cornell were unaware of such "backdoor" admissions subterfuge!

The harm to the student also occurs when the college counselor feels less responsibility to the student because someone else is doing the job. Many parents are not aware that the high school advocacy of their child makes a difference in a college's selection of freshmen. The high school college counselor is the one who will be advocating or not advocating, communicating or not communicating with the colleges. A young man from a large public high school in New York City came to see me because he didn't trust his guidance counselor to send anything in on time. He wanted the teachers to give him their recommendations and his transcript to send with his application. That doesn't work. No matter how inefficient, busy, or unfriendly the guidance

> No matter how inefficient, busy, or unfriendly the guidance counselor appears to be, seniors must make an effort to turn that relationship around and make a friend of their counselor.

counselor appears to be, seniors must make an effort to turn that relationship around and make a friend of their counselor. When a college has a question about a senior's performance or application, they do not call the coach, the favorite teacher, or the outside consultant—they call only the high school's college advisor or guidance counselor. Seniors need their high schools' advocacy. You need the high school advocacy for your child. The highest-paid consultant in the world can't get anywhere without the student's high school advocacy. I asked my colleague at a top boarding school,

"Hey, Tommy, what do you say to parents who ask you what you think of them getting an outside college consultant?" "Good," he replied, "now I won't have to worry about your son."

The greatest harm of the independent counselor, however, is that an outsider teaches a "beat the system mentality" rather than an educational process of self-assessment, research (studying all of the colleges in order to find the best match), and communication with the colleges (application, essay, interviews, and special portfolios). When the independent consultant and the parents who hire him take control of the process, they also take control *away* from the student just when the developmental task of an adolescent is best empowered by parents letting go. The college selection process is an educational process. A student's work toward creating college options teaches independence, self-reliance, and decision-making skills that build confidence, all of which young people will need when they leave home.

A student's work toward creating college options teaches independence, self-reliance, and decision-making skills that build confidence, all of which young people will need when they leave home.

Stepping outside the school system often takes away this educational opportunity for seniors. The college selection process is an adolescent's developmental task for transition from home life to campus life. This process belongs in our schools; its value is educational and personal growth. Moms can't write a note to excuse their sons from it. Dads can't pay someone to do it for their daughters. It's the place where students grow into the job. If you do go for a private consultant, let me caution you with words of wisdom: Be sure you work in partnership with your son's and daughter's guidance counselor. Be sure your son knows that the college process is his responsibility, even though he is getting help from a private consultant.

Keep in mind that your daughter's high school counselor, not the hired gun, has to be her strongest advocate to win the heart of the college admissions dean.

The difficulty for parents is that they know that the competition for college admissions is increasing. The selection process and the odds for bright, highly qualified high school students to get into America's top colleges are different from when they were applying to college in the sixties and seventies. Chances for admission are more competitive than even two years ago when an older sibling may have applied. They're especially different for students from private schools, who were often accepted into the most selective colleges by custom. Until the past decade, many public school students didn't even aspire to attend the top colleges. Most of those students didn't realize that need-based financial aid was available, thus keeping them from even dreaming that admission to our country's top universities was a real possibility. The thousands of international students who are now coming to America for their higher education must also be added to the equation.

> **If colleges were stocks I'd advise you to sell overvalued Duke and Georgetown, buy undervalued Carleton and Chicago, and hold Swarthmore, Harvard, and Princeton. Sell Amherst and Williams and buy Hamilton.**

Simply put, the fundamental law of supply and demand provides many profit-making opportunities. SAT coaching, packaging students, selling essays, and hiring college consultants outside of high school, and yes, even the publishing world and books like *Winning the Heart of the College Admissions Dean* adds up to a $500-million-a-year college admissions industry.

To maximize its profits, it is important for this industry to keep the image of a tight market in front of the public by defining "top colleges" as a very select few, rather than trumpeting the reality of the hundreds of excellent colleges available to high school seniors. Parents are led to believe that it is always better to choose Harvard, Princeton, and Stanford over Best State University because of top Ivys presumably superior education environment, better alumni connections, and more lucrative on-campus recruiting opportunities. Even though an economist at Princeton and a researcher at the Andrew W. Mellon Foundation found no economic advantage in attending a selective college, and even though the majority of top CEOs surveyed by *Fortune* in 1990 did not attend an elite college, parents still opt for the $150,000 investment at the most selective colleges in America. Even Wall Street parents don't consider overvalue when it comes to where their own daughter and son are going to college. "Now look," I often say to those Wall Street parents, "if colleges were stocks, I'd advise you to sell overvalued Duke and Georgetown, buy undervalued Carleton and Chicago, and hold Swarthmore, Harvard, and Princeton. Sell Amherst and Williams and buy Hamilton." They smile, hold everything they know, do almost no research on colleges they don't know, and buy any blue chip college they can get their hands on—no matter what the match is for their child or how globalization is changing our world. Choosing a college has become, and continues to be, big business in America.

Within this moneymaking machinery, opportunities for profit—marketing college admissions to thousands of anxious and fearful parents—have become an entrepreneur's delight. The most visible of the businesses are the SAT coaching companies, such as Kaplan and Princeton Review, who don't hesitate to promise a 100-point improvement in SAT scores.

The SAT Scare

Wanting to do what's best for your child sometimes means being sure that he gets into one or more of America's top 10 percent of the colleges, the big three hundred. For some of you, it means the big fifty. Still other parents have in mind only the big three: Harvard, Princeton, and Yale. It may sound scary at first to learn that Princeton turns down 76 percent of its applicants who scored between 750 and a perfect 800 on the SAT.

Following right after these SAT numbers is this revealing statistic: Princeton offered admission to 495 of 1,534 valedictorians of their class. Think of it. More than one thousand applicants who were number one in the high school class were sent a denial letter from Princeton. But on second thought, isn't it encouraging and refreshing to realize that your child doesn't need a perfect score and perfect grades to get in? That numbers won't do it!

When you begin to realize that it's true, the numbers won't get him or her in, then you realize that your son and daughter can concentrate on learning and doing interesting things that are unique to them rather than spending two years of Saturdays at an SAT prep course; they can be reading instead of memorizing vocabulary from flash cards. Your teenagers can be spending their time in a play or practicing cello or collecting model World War II tanks. Your children can be developing their interests and skills and sensibilities, rather than molding themselves into testing robots that won't necessarily get them where their SATs promise.

There isn't a college in the country where a motivated student with SAT scores of 650 verbal and 650 math can't do the work.

Test scores disappoint! The numbers (SAT scores and grades) your children achieve could get them into the top colleges *if* we were looking only at the qualifications necessary *to do the work* at a particular college. But we're not looking only at Allison's or Paul's ability to do the work. We may be, but the colleges aren't. The colleges are looking at thousands of applications, known as the "applicant pool," for a few hundred freshman places. They separate out interesting young people for their freshman community who are within a wide test-score range. It's the student's ability to use his or her brainpower that the college is eager to know about. What they *can* do and what they *choose* to do with all of those raw high numbers is what counts in the college deans' decisions.

There isn't a college in the country where a motivated student with SAT scores of 650 verbal and 650 math can't do the work. The last thing a college admissions dean does is compare Jane with Dick and say, "Oh these two are exactly alike except Jane is thirty points higher on her verbal, so we will take her." And yet many of the questions to college admissions deans run as if this is the basic assumption of students and their parents.

Tom Anthony, former Colgate dean, once told me, "After we select the qualifieds out, we still have four thousand applications for five hundred places, then we make a selective judgment of just what kind of brain the kid has. How does she think? What kind of a learner is he? We look for the student who can ask the best questions, not the one who can give the right answers."

The Dean's Point of View

Let's look from the college admissions dean's point of view and try to understand what they are after, in order to make sense of the competition for college admission. When I asked Harvard's Dean Fitzsimmons what he is after—what he looks at most closely—he just nodded his head as if that were the wrong question and told me, "Everything. We look at everything." That means that once a student is within a reasonable range of curriculum, grades, and SATs, the admissions dean is looking for an interesting freshman class that will be a perfect match for his particular campus culture. They consider curriculum choice; in-depth study, especially in mathematics, foreign language, and science; and the risk-taking factor, especially in areas the student isn't crazy about. As the deans read through the folders, many students just pop right up as instant superstars and fascinating applicants. It isn't so much "What's wrong with my application?" as it is a matter of what's right with the outstanding applications. Let me explain. Think of what it takes to be a champion athlete. Let's take a track star or swimmer. We can measure the numbers—height, weight, time, speed, and distance of previous events—but what we look for in a winner is also motivation, discipline, coachability, attitude about winning, ability to focus in all kinds of weather, and ability to function with tight competition on her heels. Numbers alone don't do it. Values, attitudes, and behavior have to be factored into the decision—and they are.

If the top colleges value one skill above all others, it is writing. Doesn't that make sense? After all, writing reflects how one thinks and can express oneself. Good writing means more than technically correct. An essay can be correct and very ordinary. Most writing is. Most people are. It's the extraordinary writer that the selective colleges are looking for. The written word that soars, or is inspirational or logical within a different system of reasoning from the ordinary, or creative and innovative in how students see themselves in the world. A teacher can encourage all of these qualities, but it is within the young person's experience that a few shine and stand out above all others. These are the select human beings from all over the world that get to go to the top of the top colleges. Their range of SAT scores will vary from 650 verbal to 800. A few will come in under that.

> If the top colleges value one skill above all others, it is writing.

What else are the colleges looking for? Besides finding the fascinating, curious, smart student, colleges need to fill the positions that will run the college community. As a director of admissions responding to this question put it, "If I need a quarterback, I'm going to get one!" Besides quarterbacks, those positions the admissions dean has to fill include all of the institution's priorities: legacies; leadership roles in publications, student government, racial and gender issues; children of influential and donor families; athletic teams and music groups. Admissions also has to come up with the diversity provided by underrepresented ethnic and geographical groups the world over.

America's top colleges get to choose their freshmen from thousands of interesting young people who will eventually lead the world in every imaginable field. Their abilities and sensibilities develop through opportunities they find in their family and high school communities. How high school students spend their time outside the classroom is the measure of their values. The selective college applicants are curious, disciplined young people who have already achieved in filmmaking, Olympic athletics, international church work, publishing software programs, regional political contests, poetry readings, university science labs, Broadway roles, and composing country-western music. Spending their school years distinguishing themselves and documenting their achievement in essay form is what will get your children where you wish they could go.

Family Life Is Hard to Do

Letting your child make the final decision about college on her own is often a frustrating task. Some of the difficulty is that you would do things differently than your child does them. Knowing that it's hard to keep a balance of doing it your way and encouraging them to do it their way, you might find that some of these things will help.

Open Minds Win

It turns out that in this highly competitive field the first thing to do is to broaden your own horizons concerning the hundreds of excellent colleges and universities from which your children have to choose. Research the colleges right along with them by reading *The Fiske Guide to Colleges* to get started in seeing what's out there. Try hard to keep an open mind and help your child to do the same. Try not to get stuck on "She has to go to Brown." I just can't begin to tell you how many terribly disappointed and distraught parents in April come back at Christmastime of the following year to say, "What a wonderful match Susie Q. has found at Whitman or Macalester. We are on the parent committee and let me tell you about their outreach to high schools." Try to downplay the hysteria in the media—the front-page SAT stories. Try to focus on the process your son is going through, encouraging him as he discovers what he wants and what's out there. Parents have the responsibility of keeping their child's mind open as she researches the colleges. This responsibility is harder to do than it sounds.

We all hear so much about a very few of the terrific colleges and universities in America. We can't help but think that if we know it, it must be better than one we've never heard of—after all, that's what marketing and advertising is all about! When they become aware, however, many parents can get beyond the college name and rating. They, too, start to ask, "What's it like? What's the fit? What will become of my son and daughter if they go to your school?"

Write a Letter to the Guidance Counselor

Here's an opportunity to give *your* input about your daughter; a chance to say what she's like to live with at home and how she relates to her brothers and sisters, family pet, grandparents, and neighbors; a place for you to write about her special talents, her cares and worries. Some parents have written about childhood illness, unusual emotional stress in the family (more than the regular stress that we all have), rationale for poor grades, high hopes, responsibilities their daughter and son take in the home. Write anything that will add a family dimension to the counselor's understanding of a student and that she can use in her recommendation to the colleges. Parent letters are invaluable for student descriptions.

A letter to the guidance counselor is your chance to get your message across to the college admissions dean about how unique your son is. Tell a story or relate an incident. Tell how he has overcome disappointments and what you're most proud of. Don't let the written word frighten you. You won't be graded! Use any of these ideas for your letter. Even though the counselor may not ask for a written description of your son or daughter, any counselor in the country who has to get those student recommendation letters written before November 1 and January 1 can use a parent's written statement to better describe her students. I'm going to trust that you are smart enough not to tell the counselor how to do her job and that you'll think of a natural way to get your letter to her. Remember that this counselor is your child's advocate. The better she knows him, the stronger her advocacy will be. So with your best smile, in your most off-hand manner, offer the letter with an "in case you find it helpful" kind of phrase.

Here is a parent questionnaire that a boarding school asks their parents to fill out before they meet for a college conference. This may give you some helpful ideas of what to include in a letter to your child's guidance counselor.

- ▶ **What characteristics are you especially interested in finding in a college for your son or daughter?**

- ▶ **List three adjectives which describe your son or daughter.**

- ▶ **Describe your child—her "learning style," motivation, strengths, weaknesses. What are her principal achievements?**

- ▶ **I am proud of my child because . . .**

- ▶ **Are there any family situations, medical history, special awards that we should know about which would be helpful in describing him?**

- ▶ **Will your child be applying for financial aid?**

- ▶ **How important is college prestige in your support of your child's college choice?**

- ▶ **How do you see your child distinguishing himself from his siblings or friends? In what ways is she her own person?**

If you aren't comfortable with a letter, write an outline. Tell what you most admire about your child. Describe what you like most about living with him. *Write everything you wish the college knew about your daughter or son!* If you don't have a college conference with the guidance counselor, then it's all the more important to get in your two cents. Remember that the unconscious is always at work in winning a heart, and we all like best what we know best. Be sure that the counselor knows your son and daughter best. Don't drive them crazy with information they don't want, but one letter or outline describing your child can't possibly be interpreted as too much.

The College Process Builds Character

You've heard it before and you know how important it is that your daughter and son feel free to make their own college decision in order to gain a sense of responsibility and independence. After all, they are the ones who are going to be living the consequences of their choice for four years. The college selection process is tough. It builds character. And heaven knows that students will need character to succeed in their first year away from home—your son's and daughter's first year at college.

Blessed Assurance

No matter how good you are at parenting, it's hard not to feel overwhelmed with anxiety in late March of your child's senior year. Talking to your school guidance counselor, principal, or headmaster just doesn't help for long. In fact, no one else can help because the only thing that will lessen that anxiety is the college decision letter. I tell my parents to try to change the subject in their heads—exercise, go out and run or ski or just plain walk fast. Whatever your coping mechanism is for high anxiety, get that coping machinery well oiled and in place before February and March, because every parent of a high school senior in the college selection process needs it. A sense of humor and perspective helps too, but in the college-panic months of February and March, logical solutions let us down—humor goes out the window and perspective pulls the shade. The hard truth is that blessed assurance will not be yours until the fat letter sings a YES! Winning a few hearts during the college selection process—plus your son's and daughter's heart—is the only way to go.

ABOUT THE AUTHOR

Joyce Slayton Mitchell is a Vermonter who spent two years in the Sepik area of Papua New Guinea, where she learned how to collect the data necessary to see another culture. Currently, she is the Director of College Advising at the Nightingale-Bamford School, an independent school for girls in New York City. Mitchell's mission in life is to help teenagers broaden their options as they make decisions about college and career.

Mitchell serves on the Editorial Advisory Board for the College Board's *College Board Review,* and on the school committee of *U. S. News & World Report*'s special college issue. She is the author of more than thirty-three works of nonfiction, including *College to Career: The Guide to Career Planning* (The College Board, 1994), *Winning the Chemo Battle* (W. W. Norton, 1988, 1991), *A Special Delivery: Mother–Daughter Letters From Afar* (Equilibrium Press, 2000), *Tractor-Trailer Trucker* (Tricycle Press, 2000), and *Crashed, Smashed, and Mashed: A Trip to Junkyard Heaven* (Tricycle Press, 2001).

Mitchell travels extensively throughout the United States and abroad giving workshops, lectures, and seminars on getting into college. Check out her college advice column online at www.collegeadviceUSA.com.

College Admissions Talk

College Admissions has its own language. Here are some terms you should know.

Advanced Placement (AP): College-level courses offered in high school for which students may earn college credit. Students can qualify for advanced standing when they enroll in college; students may take the AP Exams in May whether they have taken the course or not.

American College Test (ACT): A college entrance test administered by the American College Testing Corporation. Most colleges allow students to submit scores from either the ACT or SAT I. Some coaches think that their athletes score better on the ACT than the SAT because it measures achievement rather than reasoning and wrong answers are not penalized as they are on the SAT.

Arts and sciences (the liberal arts): This is the college within a university or a separate college course of study that includes the humanities, social sciences, natural sciences, mathematics, foreign languages, and fine arts. It's America's typical undergraduate college.

Block system: The academic year is divided into nine three-and-one-half-week blocks. A student takes only one course at a time, total immersion, which gives no excuses for "I have to do the other subject first." The block system appears to be a procrastinator's hell. There are no excuses. It also permits the courses to be held off campus. Colorado College has made the block system famous.

Candidates' reply date: The May 1 deadline, observed by the selective colleges by which the applicant must respond to one offer of admission, usually with a deposit. As the competition gets more fierce, the colleges hold the May 1 deposit more rigorously.

College Board: Administers the PSAT, the SAT, the SAT II, the Advanced Placement (AP) tests, the College Scholarship Service (CSS), and PRO-FILE. The SATs are developed in arrangement with the Educational Testing Service (ETS).

Common Application: The standard application form that is accepted by more than two hundred selective colleges. Often supplemented by the college's own form. Available at www.commonapp.org or in your high school guidance office. If the college has its own application form, remember the way to win the dean's heart is through his own unique application, which he designed and values. Use the Common Application when it's the only choice.

Comprehensive exams: Final tests given college seniors in some selective liberal arts colleges, usually in their major; often required to graduate.

Consortium: A group of colleges and universities that offer joint programs, cross-registration for academic course work, and coordinated social, cultural, and athletic programs to the students within the affiliated group. For example: Amherst, Hampshire, the University of Massachusetts, Mount Holyoke, and Smith are the Five College Consortium.

Co-op job: An on-the-job training program, usually related to the student's major. Often a full-time, paid job with a semester or year off campus. Internships have replaced many of the co-op jobs in the past ten years.

Core curriculum: A specified program of courses that all students must take in order to graduate. Columbia is well known for a strong core; Brown is well known for having no core.

CSS (College Scholarship Service) PROFILE: A financial aid form from the College Board that is required by many of the selective private colleges and universities for students seeking financial aid.

Deferral: Postponement of applicants for early decision or early action that will be considered within the regular applicant pool. Also a postponement for some students from the wait list to defer until the next January, February, or even for a year.

Distribution requirements: Required courses for college graduation; usually a student can choose from many courses within the categories of the humanities, social sciences, sciences, fine arts, foreign languages, and mathematics.

Demonstrated need: The difference between the family contribution as established on the Expected Family Contribution (EFC) and the total cost of attending the college.

Early Action (EA): A program whereby students receive an early admission, deferral, or denial decision in December, but are not obligated to enroll if admitted. Harvard and Chicago are best known for EA; other well-known schools with EA programs include Boston College, Georgetown, MIT, and Notre Dame. A May 1 response is required.

Early Decision (ED): A program whereby students apply by the first or middle of November and receive an early admission, deferral, or denial decision in December, and are obligated to enroll if admitted and if financial aid award is sufficient. If admitted, ED students are required to withdraw all other college applications. Increasingly colleges are offering a second or "late" early decision, with decisions given in February; some even offer a "late-late" ED.

Ethernet: A high-speed access to the Internet found on many campuses.

ETS: Education Testing Service, Princeton, NJ; develops college entrance tests for the College Board.

Expected Family Contribution (EFC): The amount that a family is expected to pay for one year of college as determined by standardized forms from FAFSA or PROFILE.

FAFSA: *See* Free Application for Federal Student Aid.

Federal methodology (FM): The method of calculating the Expected Family Contribution (EFC) that is determined only on the FAFSA and the federal aid formula.

Fee waiver: Exemptions for needy students to apply for college admission without having to pay the application fee, for the SAT I, the SAT II, and for the PROFILE.

FFS: Family Financial Statement from ACT.

Financial aid package: The combination of aid awarded by a college that may include grants, loans, and a work-study job.

Four-one-four: An academic calendar consisting of two regular four-month semesters with a short winter or January term in between.

Free Application for Federal Student Aid (FAFSA): A financial aid form produced by the federal government that is required by nearly all colleges and universities for students seeking aid, loans, or work-study jobs.

Gapping: The practice of offering less financial aid than the student's calculated need.

Graduate student: A college student who has completed the bachelor's degree and is working toward a master's or doctoral degree.

Greek system: Fraternities and sororities on campus. They are called "Greek" because their names originate from letters in the Greek alphabet.

Humanities: Courses in which the primary focus is on human culture; this includes philosophy, foreign language, religion, and literature.

Institutional methodology (IM): A method of calculating Expected Family Contribution (EFC) that includes the FAFSA and the college's own financial aid form and institutional priorities.

Interdisciplinary major: Combined majors such as political science, philosophy, and economics, or Spanish and business administration, often created and negotiated by students.

International Baccalaureate (IB): A precisely prescribed high school program originated in Geneva, Switzerland, which is available around the world. Americans can earn advanced standing in American colleges, and many fulfill the thirteenth year requirement of foreign universities.

Language requirement: A foreign language graduation requirement at many colleges. Most AP students are exempt from this requirement if their scores meet the standard of the college. Many others can place out of the requirement through examinations during freshman orientation week.

Legacy: An applicant whose parents or grandparents are graduates of a particular college. Siblings, uncles, and aunts are not usually considered legacy. Most colleges give academically qualified legacies an edge in admissions.

Liberal arts college: This is the college within a university or a separate college course of study that includes the humanities, social sciences, natural sciences, mathematics, foreign languages, and fine arts. It's America's typical undergraduate college.

Merit scholarship: A financial grant for college awarded on academic achievement or special skill and talent in an extracurricular activity in high school, rather than awarded on need. Unrelated to the National Merit Scholarship Program.

National Merit Scholarship Program: A scholarship program that begins with the scores on the Preliminary SAT (PSAT) taken in October of the junior year. Separate programs award black and Hispanic students from the same PSAT exam.

Need-blind admissions: A policy in which the applicant's ability to pay for college does not affect the admissions decision. Fewer and fewer colleges continue to subscribe to this policy.

Open admissions: A policy whereby any student with a high school diploma is accepted, usually a policy of public universities for resident students.

Parietals: Rules that govern times when students of one sex may visit dorms or floors housing the opposite sex. Out-of-fashion rule at most, but not all, colleges.

Pass-fail: An option to replace grades at some colleges to encourage students to take courses outside of their major interests and talents, and an option at some colleges for first semester of freshman year.

Preliminary SAT (PSAT): A qualifying test for the National Merit Scholarship Program from the College Board, administered in October of junior year, and often offered to tenth graders as a practice test.

Preferential packaging: A policy of awarding financial aid in which colleges offer the best aid to their most desired applicants.

PROFILE: A financial aid form from the College Board that is required by many of the selective private colleges and universities for students seeking financial aid.

PSAT: *See* Preliminary SAT.

Quad: An abbreviation of "quadrangle" found on many traditional campuses, where the classroom or dorm complexes are built on a square or rectangle with a green in the center.

Quarter system: An academic calendar of four quarters, of which three constitute a full academic year; sometimes called the Dartmouth Plan, where students must attend one summer in the four years. This system encourages students to be more creative in their off-campus time, which can come any time of year, not only in the summer.

Resident advisor (RA): A paid student personnel officer or an upperclassman living in a freshman dorm to offer support and advice to new students.

Residential college: A living unit within a larger institution that offers special academic programs to its students; best models at Rice and Yale. In public universities, a residential college is also called a living/learning community.

Rolling admissions: An admissions policy by which a college evaluates and decides upon applicants as soon as the application is complete. Colleges often promise a decision within six weeks. Public universities are often rolling, although they often hold places until April for out-of-state students, and the dates tend to vary each year.

SAR: *See* Student Aid Report.

SAT I and II: The most widely used college entrance examinations administered by the College Board and created by Educational Testing Service (ETS). The SAT I: Reasoning Test is a three-hour test that measures verbal and math logic. The SAT II: Subject Tests are one-hour tests measuring achievement in a particular course of study.

Score Choice: An option for students taking the SAT II tests whereby students can hold their scores until they know what they are before releasing them to the colleges. There is no Score Choice option for the SAT I.

Semester system: Most American colleges are on the semester system, with two semesters constituting a full academic year, with the summer off.

Social sciences: College courses that deal with human society, including anthropology, economics, history, political science, psychology, and sociology.

Student Aid Report (SAR): The form sent to families after filing their FAFSA form that tells the student the Expected Family Contribution (EFC).

Teaching assistant (TA): A graduate student who teaches undergraduates, and/or holds smaller discussion sections for a professor's large lectures.

Three-two program (3-2): A program in which students study three years in a liberal arts college followed by two at a specialized school, such as engineering, nursing, or business administration.

Trimesters: The academic calendar divided into three equal terms to constitute a full year.

Undergraduate: A college student working toward a bachelor's degree; usually a four-year program.

Wait list: The list of students who are qualified to attend, but not yet accepted. Also called late decision, many students get into the college they most want to attend from the wait list. It is also used for political reasons, so that the dean of admissions doesn't have to deny a legacy or donor family.

Work-study: A federally funded program whereby students are given campus jobs as part of their financial package. Students must fill out the FAFSA form in order to get a work-study position.

Yield: The percentage of the accepted students who enrolled at a particular college. Some say that admissions are driven by yield, because colleges are often rated by how many students enroll from the accepted list.

APPENDIX B

Annotated Resources

Books

The Fiske Guide to Colleges, latest edition, by Edward B. Fiske (Random House). The best essays on the market describing the campus culture of about three hundred colleges. Don't take the ratings and SAT scores needed to get in too seriously. It's the three-page description of each college by a former *New York Times* education editor that is crucial for you to have an overall understanding of what's out there in American higher education. If you have money for only one college description guide, *Fiske* is the one to buy! The guide describes the college's strongest departments and majors, the quality of academic and social life, and it gives you Web sites and e-mail addresses. You will also want to look carefully at the "overlaps." Those are the other colleges and universities to which a particular college's applicants are also applying in greatest numbers and represent its major competition. For example, if one of your choices is Wisconsin's Beloit College, then you will see that two of the overlaps are Ripon and Lawrence, both of which have many of the same qualities. Check 'em out! If Bucknell seems like a terrific match for you, then check out *Fiske's* overlaps and you will find Lafayette, Lehigh, and Penn State. Although Penn State is a state university and much bigger, nevertheless, it has qualities (geography has to be one of them!) that attract like applicants. One more: Let's say you've checked it out and you are crazy about Notre Dame. Looking at the overlaps, you will find two other Catholic universities, Boston College and Georgetown; you will also find Duke, Northwestern, and Michigan. *Fiske* gives the answer to your questions about interviews: Are they on campus or with alumni, required or optional, evaluated or not? All-important information for the applicants.

The Insider's Guide to the Colleges, latest edition *(Yale Daily News).*
Published by students for students. Don't apply to college without reading
this guide! Your parents won't necessarily like it—it's heavy on the social
life factors of college life. By now, you have learned to judge your collection of data by where it comes from. *Insider's* is important to you, and I
know that you will balance what you read with *Fiske* and with *Colleges
That Change Lives* (see page 180) if any college on your list is one of the
forty cited. Because *Insider's* is student biased; it is definitely the next best
thing to being there. Daily college life and campus culture are the most
crucial components of the college; if you don't fit in, you won't stay. The
combination of educator *Fiske* and student *Insider's* is worth twenty visits
to the college campus. Be sure to get an idea of "what it's like" to be on
campus from this guide. Again, about three hundred colleges are
described—the top 10 percent of U.S. colleges. There are a few different
colleges in *Fiske* and *Insider's,* as personal opinion varies, but for the most
part they overlap. Some of the data from *Insider's* that you won't find as easily anywhere else are percent of public school students, percent in fraternities, numbers of transfers, most popular majors (not best, most popular),
percent of students living on campus, retention rate (the percentage of students who stay for sophomore year). All the college Web sites are listed.
There's also a wonderfully fun section, FYI, asking, "What should be the
campus mascot, but isn't? What to avoid in the dining hall? What is a typical weekend schedule? What celebrity would most likely fit in at your
school? What is the most popular beverage on campus?" Now where else
could you ever find such an interesting order of information? The editors
of the *Insider's Guide* definitely had at least a minor, if not a major, in
anthropology! It's all the stuff that you need to know for your long list,
before you even think of choosing your final eight. If you haven't yet
bought this book, I'll give you the answers to the above FYI for Lewis and
Clark, Portland, Oregon: (a) mascot: a hippie driving a Range Rover; (b)
food to avoid: lentil and loaf; (c) weekend: movies or bars in Portland,
listening to a live band or two, catching a party on Saturday night. Sunday

is the day for recovery, remorse, regret, and reality; (d) beverage: Henry Weinhard's Amber Ale or Odwalla Juices. See what I mean? Don't miss it!

The College Handbook, latest edition (The College Board). One of the most accurate and up-to-date "big" college guides available. The College Board collects the data, including which SAT tests are required by each college, each year from their own membership. Every college in the country is in this guide. *Fiske* and *Insider's* describe 10 percent of the most selective and interesting colleges in America. Those three hundred colleges, along with the other 90 percent of American colleges, will be cited in *The College Handbook.* Be sure and read the Student Life section; if you plan to be a residential student, check out the percentage of students living in the dorms.

The Complete Book of Catholic Colleges by Ed Custard and Dan Saraceno (Princeton Review, 1997). There are many more Catholic colleges than the high-profile Georgetown, Notre Dame, Holy Cross, and Boston College. For an informative guide on all of the Catholic colleges in America, here is a book that has the answers.

Hillel Guide to Jewish Campus Life by Ruth Fredman Cernea (Random House, 2000). If you're Jewish or have a Jewish heritage, find out how many Jewish students are on campus before you decide to go there. You may like very few or a lot; the point is to know if you are one of a crowd or if you will be known only as the Jewish kid on campus. This guide also describes the Jewish community outside the college, which often invites college students to their homes for holidays.

African American Student's College Guide (John Wiley & Sons, 2000). Here is the best source for in-depth profiles of the top one hundred colleges for African American students. The guide comes from the nation's top African American college guidance service, Black Excel: The College Help Network. It includes insider tips for black students on the admissions process, how to choose a school, writing the essay, and paying for college.

The Multicultural Student's Guide to Colleges by Robert Mitchell (Noonday Press, 1996). What every African American, Asian American, and Hispanic applicant needs to know about America's top colleges. Includes campus culture, racial integration, ratio of men to women, numbers of multicultural professors tenured—the best guide of its kind.

Colleges That Change Lives by Loren Pope (Penguin Books, 2000). A fascinating description of forty outstanding American colleges with strong academic and interesting programs where students get engaged with learning and issues beyond the usual collegiate level of commitment. Selectivity is often less than better-known colleges; in other words, here is a list of many undervalued colleges that the author knows enough to value! You should too. Look them up! Allegheny, Antioch, Austin, Bard, Beloit, Birmingham-Southern, Centre, Clark University, Cornell College, Denison, Earlham, Eckerd, Emory and Henry, Evergreen, Franklin and Marshall, Goucher, Grinnell, Guilford, Hampshire, Hendrix, Hiram, Hope, Juniata, Kalamazoo, Knox, Lawrence, Lynchburg, Marlboro, Millsaps, Ohio Wesleyan, Reed, Rhodes, St. Andrews Presbyterian, St. John's (MD and NM), Southwestern (TX), Western Maryland, Wheaton (IL), Whitman, College of Wooster.

International Student Handbook (The College Board, 2000). The most official guide for international students written in cooperation among the College Board's Office of International Education, U.S. government agencies involved with international educational exchange, overseas educational advisors, and international admission officers at U.S. colleges. Everything international students need to know about ESL programs, TOEFL scores, international testing centers, application deadlines, financial aid, housing, and a complete worldwide list of international advising centers.

Web Sites

College advice: Read Joyce Slayton Mitchell's *Ask JSM* and send in your college questions to www.collegeadviceUSA.com.

College Board: www.collegeboard.com. You can register for the SATs, download the CSS PROFILE financial aid form, do a college search, a scholarship search, ask questions and find test preparation online.

College Edge: www.collegedge.com. Besides a college search, this site includes a scholarship search.

Common applications: www.commomapp.org. Download the common app from this site.

Educational Testing Service: www.ets.org. Get the SAT and TOEFL test dates as well as practice questions that you need for studying. Register for these tests through the College Board Web site above.

Financial-aid site: www.finaid.org. The best site for all of your financial-aid questions.

Free Application for Federal Student Aid (FAFSA) form: www.fafsa.ed.gov. Every college requires this form for student aid and work-study programs.

Princeton Review: www.review.com; www.weapply.com. The easiest online application source, and one of the best college search programs.

PROFILE form: www.collegeboard.org

TOEFL Online: www.toefl.org. Register, find out the test dates, and get practice questions online.

United States Department of Education: www.ed.gov. Request *The Student Guide: Financial Aid from the U.S. Department of Education* and your FAFSA form.

U.S. News and World Report: www.usnews.com. Learn how colleges are rated and use what is important to you.

Winning the Heart of the College Admissions Dean: An Expert's Advice for Getting into College: www.collegeadviceUSA.com. Send your college admissions questions and comments to *Ask JSM*, the twice-weekly college-advice column.

APPENDIX C

Top 101 American Colleges

Amherst College, Amherst, MA 01002   www.amherst.edu

Bard College, Annandale-on-Hudson, NY 12504   www.bard.edu

Barnard College, New York, NY 10027   www.barnard.edu

Bates College, Lewiston, ME 04240   www.bates.edu

Beloit College, Beloit, WI 53511   www.beloit.edu

Berkeley, University of California at, Berkeley, CA 94720
   www.berkeley.edu

Boston College, Chestnut Hill, MA 02467   www.bc.edu

Bowdoin College, Brunswick, ME 04011   www.bowdoin.edu

Brandeis, Waltham, MA 02454   www.brandeis.edu

Brown University, Providence, RI 02912   www.brown.edu

Bryn Mawr College, Bryn Mawr, PA 19010   www.brynmawr.edu

Bucknell University, Lewisburg PA 17837   www.bucknell.edu

California Institute of Technology, Pasadena, CA 91125
   www.caltech.edu

Carleton College, Northfield, MN 55057   www.carleton. edu

Carnegie Mellon University, Pittsburgh, PA 15213   www.cmu.edu

Case Western Reserve University, Cleveland, OH 44106
   www.cwru.edu

Centre College, Danville, KY 40422   www.centre.edu

Chicago, University of, Chicago, IL   www.chicago.edu

Claremont McKenna College, Claremont, CA 91711
   www.mckenna.edu

Colby College, Waterville, ME 04901   www.colby.edu

Colgate University, Hamilton, NY 13346   www.colgate.edu

Colorado College, Colorado Springs, CO 80903
   www.coloradocollege.edu

Columbia University, New York, NY 10027   www.columbia.edu

Connecticut College, New London, CT 06320   www.conncoll.edu

Cooper Union, New York, NY 10003   www.cooper.edu

Cornell University, Ithaca, NY 14850   www.cornell.edu

Dartmouth College, Hanover, NH 03755   www.dartmouth.edu

Davidson College, Davidson, NC 28036   www.davidson.edu

Denison University, Granville, OH 43023   www.denison.edu

Dickinson College, Carlisle, PA 17013   www.dickinson.edu

Duke University, Durham, NC 27708   www.duke.edu

Emory University, Atlanta, GA 30322   www.emory.edu

Evergreen State University, Olympia, WA 98505   www.evergreen.edu

Franklin and Marshall College, Lancaster, PA 17604   www.fandm.edu

Georgetown University, Washington, DC 20057
   www.georgetowncollege.edu

Georgia Institute of Technology, Atlanta, GA 30332   www.gatech.edu

Grinnell College, Grinnell, IA 50112   www.grinnell.edu

Hamilton College, Clinton, NY 13323   www.hamilton.edu

Harvard University, Cambridge, MA 02138   www.harvard.edu

Harvey Mudd College, Claremont, CA 91711   www.hmc.edu

Haverford College, Haverford, PA 19041   www.haverford.edu

Holy Cross, College of the, Worcester, MA 01610   www.holycross.edu

Indiana University, Bloomington, IN 47405   www.iub.edu

Johns Hopkins University, Baltimore, MD 21218   www.jhu.edu

Kenyon College, Gambier, OH 43022   www.kenyon.edu

Lafayette College, Easton, PA 18042   www.lafayette.edu

Lehigh University, Bethlehem, PA 18015   www.lehigh.edu

Lewis and Clark College, Portland, OR 97210   www.clark.edu

Los Angeles, University of California at (UCLA), Los Angeles, CA
   90095   www.ucla.edu

Macalester College, St. Paul, MN 55105   www.macalester.edu

Maryland, University of, College Park, MD 20742   www.umd.edu

Massachusetts Institute of Technology, Cambridge, MA 02139
www.mit.edu

Michigan, University of, Ann Arbor, MI 33124   www.umich.edu

Middlebury College, Middlebury, VT 05753   www.middlebury.edu

Mount Holyoke College, South Hadley, MA 01075
www.mtholyoke.edu

New York University, New York, NY 10012   www.nyu.edu

North Carolina at Chapel Hill, University of, Chapel Hill, NC 25799
www.unc.edu

Northwestern University, Evanston, IL 60208   www.nwu.edu

Notre Dame, University of, Notre Dame, IN 46556   www.nd.edu

Oberlin College, Oberlin, OH 44074   www.oberlin.edu

Occidental College, Los Angeles, CA 90041   www.oxy.edu

Pennsylvania, University of, Philadelphia, PA 19104   www.upenn.edu

Pitzer College, Claremont, CA 91711   www.pitzer.edu

Pomona College, Claremont, CA 91711   www.pomona.edu

Princeton University, Princeton, NJ 08544   www.princeton.edu

Reed College, Portland, OR 97202   www.reed.edu

Rensselaer Polytechnic Institute, Troy, NY 12180   www.rpi.edu

Rhodes College, Memphis, TN 38112   www.rhodes.edu

Rice University, Houston, TX 77005   www.rice.edu

Rochester, University of, Rochester, NY 15627   www.rochester.edu

Rutgers University, Brunswick, NJ 08901   www.rutgers.edu

St. John's College, Annapolis, MD 21402   www.sjca.edu; and Santa Fe,
NM 87501   www.sjcsf.edu

San Diego, University of California at, La Jolla, CA 92093
www.ucsd.edu

Santa Cruz, University of California at, Santa Cruz, CA 95064
www.ucsc.edu

Scripps College, Claremont, CA 91711   www.scrippscol.edu

Sewanee (University of the South), Sewanee, TN 37383
www.sewanee.edu

Smith College, Northampton, MA 01063   www.smith.edu

Stanford University, Stanford, CA 94305   www.stanford.edu

SUNY, Binghamton, Binghamton, NY 13902   www.binghamton.edu

Swarthmore College, Swarthmore, PA 19081   www.swarthmore.edu

Syracuse University, Syracuse, NY 13244   www.syr.edu

Texas, University of, Austin, TX 78712   www.utexas.edu

Trinity College, Hartford, CT 06106   www.trincoll.edu

Tufts University, Medford, MA 02155   www.tufts.edu

Tulane University, New Orleans, LA 70118   www.tulane.edu

Union College, Schenectady, NY 12308   www.union.edu

Vanderbilt University, Nashville, TN 37240   www.vanderbilt.edu

Vassar College, Poughkeepsie, NY 12604   www.vassar.edu

Vermont, University of, Burlington, VT 05405   www.uvm.edu

Virginia, University of, Charlottesville, VA 22904   www.virginia.edu

Wake Forest University, Winston-Salem, NC 27106   www.wfu.edu

Washington and Lee University, Lexington, VA 24450   www.wlu.edu

Washington University, St. Louis, MO 93130   www.wustl.edu

Wellesley College, Wellesley, MA 02481   www.wellesley.edu

Wesleyan University, Middletown, CT 06457   www.wesleyan.edu

Whitman College, Walla Walla, WA 99362   www.whitman.edu

William and Mary, College of, Williamsburg, VA 23187   www.wm.edu

Williams College, Williamstown, MA 01267   www.williams.edu

Wisconsin, University of, Madison, WI 53706   www.wisc.edu

Yale University, New Haven, CT 06520   www.yale.edu

Yeshiva University, New York, NY 10033   www.yu.edu

Sources: *U.S. News and World Report* (2001), *The Fiske Guide to Colleges* (2001), and the author.

INDEX